THE COMING ERA OF PEACE

MARIAN APPARITIONS PREDICTING OUR TIMES

BY

DAVID G. SMITHSON, MD

Copyright © 2023 David G Smithson, MD
All rights reserved.

*Dedication to the Sacred Heart of Jesus
and the Immaculate Heart of Mary*

Acknowledgments

I would like to thank my wife, Mollie, for her love and support throughout this project. I also appreciate the support and input from my brother, Doug, and my sister, Kathy. I would further like to thank both of my priest nephews, Fr. Jason and Fr. Aaron regarding their excellent and detailed input and ideas.

Thank you to the following beta readers for their helpful input: Polly Rupp, Karen Sutherland, Connie Euston and Tom Arnold.

I appreciate the support of the Knights of Columbus council #12546 from Bucyrus, KS, including especially Tom McGuire, Grand Knight, Anthony Battaglia, Mike Gollum, Dan Ritter, Bob Triano and Lenny Vohs.

Thank you to Lari Prilliman for her ongoing and excellent administrative support. Thanks to Kari Sherman from Your Catholic Editor for her creative insights and excellent editing services.

Preface

As faithful Catholics looking around at the world today, it's hard not to question whether we are approaching, or are already in, the end times. Attacks on the traditional family, Christian values, and basic moral issues abound. The book you are holding in your hands came to fruition because of my own journey of trying to understand the "signs of the times" we are living in. I am not a theologian nor a historian, but merely an interested lay Catholic.

The opinions expressed herein are largely based on multiple approved Marian apparitions, which are included in the back of this book. Every effort was made in the research undertaken to be truthful and transparent. It is my hope that by sharing the message of these apparitions and endeavoring to interpret them, that you will grow in faith, courage, and hope, realizing that each of you have been specifically chosen to live at this point in history, for such a time as this. In the end, it is deferred to church theologians, historians and pastors to analyze the statements and opinions thus generated.

Chapter 1

Introduction

It is no news to those reading this, that we are living in tumultuous times. If you're familiar with the book of Revelation, you know that there will come a time when things on Earth get very, very bad. But where are we on this course of End Times prophecy and what does the Church have to say about these matters? Is there any information out there, besides the Bible and the writings of saints, to help us?

In our era, there have been a large and increasing number of individuals claiming to have had encounters with, or experienced apparitions of, the Blessed Virgin Mary. Many of these messages carry prognostications for the times that we are living in. As the faithful, we are left with the challenging proposition of what to make of all of these apparent visits from heaven, when the vast majority are still awaiting approval of the Church.

The Bible tells us: "Do not despise the words of prophets, but test everything; hold fast to what is good…"[1] So how do we "test" the abundant apparitions of our day? How do we know if the messages by a specific visionary are "good," as described above, or even legitimate?

---

[1] Thessalonians 5:20-21

Many of the messages of these modern visionaries concern future events, which leaves us wondering whether these events will actually come to pass. Should we blindly believe them all, ignore them, or believe some and not others? By what criteria do we decide this? Do we look at the surrounding miraculous events, try to assess the holiness of the alleged visionaries, or look at the fruits of the apparition? How can we know we are getting the correct information when attempting to make these judgements? All these questions can leave our heads spinning!

The reality is, we lay people are not qualified to complete investigations on this matter and the Church must be prudent in her approach. There are so many factors involved in assessing the validity of an apparent Marian apparition, and that job should be left to the appropriate experts.

Keeping this in mind, I wondered what I could find out about our current times by looking only at the apparitions which have already been approved. By investigating those with Church approval, I had the security of knowing I was dealing with visions and messages that have actually come from the Blessed Virgin Mary. They have met the criteria of the Church itself and thus have been deemed worthy of belief by the faithful.

In my search for information on approved Marian apparitions, the best source I found was EWTN's The Miracle Hunter[2], which claims to be "The Internet's Top Resource for Miracles." In an organized and easy-to-read format, their website includes information on apparitions, miraculous images, eucharistic miracles, stigmata

---

[2] Miraclehunter.com

occurrences, and incorruptibles. The Marian apparitions are categorized by type of approval, and for my investigation I elected to focus on the 25 "Vatican Approved" and "Bishop Approved" ones.

Because my goal was to look at what Marian apparitions show us about the End Times, it made sense to only include the ones that contained future predictions for our era. This allowed me to narrow the original list of 25 down to these nine:

1. Guadalupe, Mexico, Our Lady of Guadalupe (1531)
2. Quito, Ecuador, Our Lady of Good Success (1594)
3. La Salette, France, Our Lady of La Salette (1846)
4. Fatima, Portugal, Our Lady of Fatima/Our Lady of the Rosary (1917)
5. Akita, Japan, Our Lady of Akita (1973)
6. Betania, Venezuela, Reconciler of People and Nations (1976)
7. Cuapa, Nicaragua, Our Lady of Cuapa (1980)
8. Kibeho, Rwanda, Mother of the Word (1981)
9. San Nicolas, Argentina, Our Lady of the Rosary (1983)

(Note: For more information on why these nine were chosen, see Appendix 1. Appendices 2-10 contain more information about the nine apparitions chosen, including a timeline of the approved apparition and a synopsis or sampling of the main messages and/or events by Our Lady.)

Besides the nine approved Marian apparitions, I will also discuss the well-known vision of Pope Leo XIII, from the late 1800s. This documented vision resulted in Pope Leo XIII writing the Saint Michael prayer for protection against the devil, which spread worldwide. In Appendix 11, you can find a separate summary of this event as an additional quick reference.

Moving forward, we will use the aforementioned apparitions and vision to attempt to further assess important questions concerning our times. Some of these questions include:

- In what way did the Blessed Virgin Mary actually foretell our era and how specific was she?
- Why do the times we are living in seem so tumultuous?
- Are we currently living in the end of an era or at the end of the world?
- What is involved with this current troubled era and how long will it last?
- Why has the King of France been used as an analogy?

Mary also talked about a period of peace, especially as foretold at Fatima, so we will also investigate the following:

- Did this era of peace already occur or is it yet to come?
- What are the benefits of the Fatima consecrations that have been done?
- What is (or was) involved in this noted period of peace?

- What do the other approved apparitions add that can further increase our understanding of this topic?
- If it is in the future, do we know how long the era of peace is going to be? What will it be like?
- What happens to the devil during this peaceful era? Is he banished to hell? If he is not banished to hell, how can there be peace?
- As we continue today onward, what are we to do?

There is much to consider and much to discuss. But before we get into the approved Marian apparitions and their predictions, it is important to lay down some basic groundwork about how God communicates with humanity and the special role of the Blessed Mother. This will then help us in further understanding the role of Mary in reaching out to her people.

Chapter 2

A Heavenly Advocate

Our God has a history of direct involvement in the earthly lives of his people. This goes back as far as the very beginning of mankind. After breathing life into Adam, God later walked in the garden with Adam and Eve. When mankind had subsequently turned evil, God gave Noah very specific guidance regarding the building of the ark. With Abraham, God called him to travel to a new land, changed his name (from Abram to Abraham) and his wife's name (from Sarai to Sarah), and miraculously gave them a son (Isaac) in their old age. He told Abraham, "Look up at the sky and count the stars if you can. Just so, he added, will your descendants be."[3] And true to his word, the tribe of Abraham grew in numbers, starting with Jacob and expanding, eventually becoming a nation under Moses.

While God has direct involvement in our earthly lives, he also makes it clear that he is the God of the living and not the God of the dead. While appearing to Moses as the burning bush, the following conversation occurs: "God said, 'Do not come near! Remove your sandals from your feet for the place where you stand is holy

---

[3] Genesis 15:5

ground.' He continued, 'I am the God of your father, the God of Abraham, the God of Isaac, and the God of Jacob.'"[4] Note he does not say, "I *was* the God of Abraham, the God of Isaac, and the God of Jacob," but that "I *am* the God of Abraham, the God of Isaac, and the God of Jacob."[5]

He then gave the call and commission to Moses:

> I have witnessed the affliction of my people in Egypt and have heard their cry against their taskmasters so I know well what they are suffering. Therefore I have come down to rescue them from the power of the Egyptians and lead them up from that land into a good and spacious land, a land flowing with milk and honey ... Now indeed the outcry of the Israelites has reached me and I have seen how the Egyptians are oppressing them. Now go! I am sending you to Pharaoh to bring my people, the Israelites, out of Egypt.[6]

We can see how God knows, from on high, exactly what is taking place on earth. He witnessed the affliction of the Israelites and heard their cry. He became directly involved through one of them – Moses – to rescue his people. We can glean from this several obvious (and important) principles for us moving forward: (1) He knows exactly what is taking place in our world; (2) He does listen to us; (3) He utilizes human agents (in this case Moses) to carry out his plans.

---

[4] Exodus 3:5-6
[5] Italics added for emphasis
[6] Exodus 3:7-10

After rescuing the people under Moses from the Egyptians and the prolonged wandering in the desert (with manna from heaven for nourishment), God enables Joshua to overtake the Promised Land. In the person of Joshua, He again utilizes a human agent that will do his will in carrying out his plan.

The Judges then begin leading Israel followed by Saul (the first king) before King David. David has a noted special place in God's heart: "After removing Saul, he made David their king. God testified concerning him: 'I have found David, son of Jesse, a man after my own heart; He will do everything I want him to do.'"[7] This is further expressed in Ezekiel: "My servant David will be king over them and they will all have one shepherd. They will follow my laws and be careful to keep my decrees."[8]

We can see through David, that when a person is truly open to God's will, God can more effectively utilize that person as his instrument.

David and Bathsheba have a son, Solomon, and David has a long reign under God's guidance. As 1 Chronicles 28 tells us: "He died at a good old age having enjoyed long life, wealth and honor. His son Solomon succeeded him as king."

Now King Solomon asked for the gift of wisdom during his younger years, and with it came immense wealth beyond imagination. Through God's guidance came the building of the massive and marvelous Jewish temple. King Solomon had many wives, as was characteristic of the polygamy of the Davidic kingdom.

---

[7] Acts 13:22
[8] Ezekiel 37:24

But Solomon, of course, only had one mother and Bathsheba was given the very important place of queen mother. So there really was no "queen" of the Davidic kingdom, but instead there was the major influence of, and respect for, the queen mother. This could best be exemplified by the following quote from 1 Kings 2:19-20:

> So Bathsheba went to King Solomon, to speak to him on behalf of Adonijah, and the king rose to meet her and bowed down to her. Then he sat on his throne and had a seat brought for the king's mother, and she sat on his right. Then she said, 'I have one small request to make of you; do not refuse me.' And the king said to her: 'Make your request, my mother, for I will not refuse you.'

So we can see through this exchange that even as king with immense wealth, power and prestige, that Solomon bows as his mother enters. Bathsheba then sits at the king's right hand, which had great significance; in the Bible the right hand is the place of ultimate honor. In this way, the queen mother sitting at the king's right hand symbolizes that she does have a share in the royal authority of the king, and as such, she holds the second most important position in the entire kingdom.

The passage regarding Bathsheba above also shows how the queen mother served as an advocate for the people, and in this way would present petitions to the king. In 1 Kings 2:17, Adonijah gives a petition to Bathsheba and asks her to take it to the king. Upon doing this, Adonijah says to her, "Pray ask King Solomon – he will not refuse you –

to give me Abishag the Shunamite as my wife."[9] This request shows that Adonijah recognizes the incredible influence that Bathsheba has over King Solomon, and demonstrates Bathsheba's role as an intercessor between the people and the king.

We see further involvement of God when he prepares his chosen people for the coming of the ultimate God-Man himself, the Messiah and Savior, Jesus Christ. He utilizes prophets to prepare the way, including Isaiah, who proclaims this famous prophecy,

> Listen, oh house of David! Is it not enough for you to weary humans? Must you also weary my God? Therefore the Lord himself will give you this sign, the virgin shall be with child, and bear a son, and shall name him Emmanuel, which means 'God is with us!'[10]

We later see this fulfilled in the very familiar Annunciation reading,

> The angel Gabriel was sent from God to a town of Galilee called Nazareth, to a virgin betrothed to a man named Joseph, of the house of David, and the virgin's name was Mary. And coming to her, he said, 'Hail, full of grace! The Lord is with you.' But she was greatly troubled at what was said and pondered what sort of greeting this might be. Then the angel said to her, 'Do not be afraid, Mary, for you have found favor with God. Behold, you will conceive in your womb and bear

---

[9] 1 Kings 2:17
[10] Isaiah 7:13-14

a son, and you shall name him Jesus. He will be great and will be called Son of the Most High and the Lord God will give him the throne of David his father and he will rule over the house of Jacob forever and of his kingdom there will be no end'[11]

We see this prophecy fulfilled as Jesus eventually sits at the throne of David his father; his kingdom will have no end. We can also see from this how Mary is the Queen Mother and is thus given the sovereign prerogative of the Queen Mother. It explains her role as Queen of Heaven. She holds the second most important position in the kingdom of heaven, second only to the King. It also helps explains her role as an intercessor for the people.

So we can add to what we previously discussed: (1) God knows exactly what is taking place in our world; (2) He does listen to us; (3) He utilizes human agents to carry out his plans; (4) He prepared the way (utilizing prophets) for the sending of his son, Jesus, as the Messiah and Savior, and the King forever; (5) Mary is the Queen Mother and receives sovereign prerogatives as the Queen of Heaven and intercessor for the people.

It is in this role, as the Queen of Heaven and as intercessor for the people, that the Virgin Mary continues to visit us. It is because of her role as Mother to us all, that she has made appearances from heaven to her people here on earth. It is her approved apparitions, as introduced last chapter and as documented in the back of this book, that have predictions for our day and time that we should pay attention to.

The first such appearances that were officially

---

[11] Luke 1: 26-33

approved and that have specific predictions or implications for our era started back in the 1500s.[12] But before we discuss these and their ramifications, we need to recognize the pertinent historical context within which they occurred. As we shall see, the Blessed Mother's messages are often in response to society's changes in peoples, nations, or in the world.

---

[12] Our Lady of Guadalupe (1531) – see Appendix 2, and Our Lady of Good Success, Quito Ecuador (1594) – see Appendix 3

Chapter 3

THE BACKDROP

The first approved Marian apparitions started back in the 1500s, and since then, further apparitions have intermittently occurred up until our present age. Obviously, a lot has changed in the world throughout that time. Various social movements have occurred, political changes have been seen within multiple nations, and especially in the last century, tremendous advancements in technology are noted. With this in mind, Our Lady's messages throughout the centuries have at certain times focused on a specific social movement or a specific country.

One social movement specifically referenced by Our Lady is Freemasonry. When she appeared as Our Lady of Good Success in Quito, Ecuador (1594), she took a strong stand against it, just like many popes have throughout history. Similarly, a nation specifically referenced by Our Lady in further exemplifying this concept is Russia, especially by Our Lady of Fatima. (The whole issue regarding the papal consecration of Russia to Mary's Immaculate Heart will be touched on in a later chapter.)

To better understand both of these appearances, the historical context of the movement of Freemasonry and the nation of Russia are important to consider. Thus, I would like to briefly look more closely at both of them, while also examining recent widespread societal changes and how the Catholic Church has fared during this timeframe. These will be important in helping us better grasp the intent and purpose of Our Lady's timely apparitions.

Let's begin with a brief look at Freemasonry. Freemasonry, as a secret society, was formally founded in 1717 with the premier Grand Lodge of England.[13] Ever since, Freemasonry has been a source of conflict with the Catholic Church, and there have been many popes that have given strong statements in this regard. A helpful reference to this is the article, *Papal Condemnations of the Lodge* by William J. Whalen.[14] In this article, Whalen noted:

> No one could accuse the Catholic Church of disguising the antipathy to freemasonry. Scarcely 20 years after the organization of modern masonry in 1717, Pope Clement XII forbade membership in the lodge and since then seven other popes have warned the faithful against the dangers of Masonic and naturalism to the Christian faith…
>
> …Masonry constitutes a religion of naturalism which considers the basic Christian doctrines of the Trinity, the Incarnation, the Atonement, the necessity of baptism and the role of the church in the plan of salvation to be quite incidental. The lodge furthermore exacts a series of oaths from its

---

[13] History.com
[14] *Papal Condemnations of the Lodge* by William J. Whalen, EWTN.com, 1996

candidates which cannot be called valid extrajudicial oaths; those who swear such oaths agreeing to the most horrible self-mutilation in order to protect a few passwords and secret grips are objectively guilty of either vain or rash swearing. Third, the Masonic Order has historically sought to destroy the Catholic Church and to substitute a purely secular society. Posing as non-partisan in religious affairs, the lodge plumps for abolishment of parochial schools, easy divorce laws, cremation, suppression of religious orders especially the Society of Jesus and a separation of Church and State never envisioned by the framers of the First Amendment…

Pope Clement directed his bull (April 28, 1738) against… sponsored Masonic lodges within his domain … Pius VII (1821), Leo XII (1825), Pius VIII (1829), and Gregory XVI (1832) issued bulls against Freemasonry and the host of secret societies which were infesting the continent and thriving on intrigue, assassination and subversion. Free thinkers flocked to the lodges as the natural base from which to attack church and state. … Pope Pius IX issued six bulls on freemasonry between 1846 and 1873. His 1865 allocution pointed out: 'Among the numerous machination and artifices by which the enemies of the Christian name have tried to attack the Church of God and sought to shake it and besiege it by efforts superfluous in truth must undoubtably be reckoned that perverse society of men called Masonic, which at first confined to darkness and obscurity now comes into light for the common ruin of religion and human society.'

The author, Mr. Whalen goes on,

One of the greatest modern popes, Leo XIII, was also one of masonry's staunchest foes. ... In his 1884 encyclical, Pope Leo indicates that the human race is divided into two opposing camps, one under God and the other under Satan. 'At every period of time each has been in conflict with the other with a variety and multiplicity of weapons and of warfare, although not always with equal ardor and assault. At this period, however, the partisans of evil seem to be combining together and to be struggling with united vehemence led on or assisted by that strongly organized and widespread association called the Freemasons. ...' Of course, the Holy Father did not mean that all Masons are wicked and all Christians saintly. He is speaking of the spirit of the Church and the spirit of Masonic naturalism as unalterably opposed to one another...

Pope Leo continued his fight against Freemasonry and his final word was delivered in 1902. The Church then stated its official position prohibiting membership in the lodge in the Code of Canon Law issued by Benedict XV in 1917."[15]

---

[15] *Papal Condemnations of the Lodge*, William J. Whalen, EWTN.com, 1996

While the Catholic Church was trying to counter Freemasonry as noted above, communist thought was developing, which would soon play out in a major way on the world's stage. Let's next look briefly at the birth of this communist thought and it's development. A limited timeline of Communist Russia's history and growth, directly from History.com, is included below.[16] This information will be important in our ongoing discussions throughout the rest of this book:

Soviet Union Emerges From October Revolution

- **February 21, 1848:** German economist and philosopher Karl Marx (with Friedrich Engels) publish *The Communist Manifesto.*
- **November 7, 1917:** The Bolsheviks, ascribing to Marxism, seize power during Russia's October Revolution. Vladimir Lenin is at the helm and uses military force. It's during this period the Red Terror (executions of the Czar's officials), prisoner-of-war labor camps, and other police state tactics are established.

---

[16] All timeline information is from https://www.history.com/topics/european-history/communism-timeline; some of it is directly quoted.

Communism Takes Hold in China and Beyond

- **July 1, 1921:** Inspired by the Russian Revolution, the Communist Party of China is formed.

- **January 21, 1924:** Lenin dies at age 54 of a stroke, and Joseph Stalin, who had served as Lenin's general secretary, eventually takes over official rule of the Soviet Union until his death in 1953 from a brain hemorrhage. He industrialized the century through a state-controlled economy, but it led to famine. Under his regime, detractors were deported or imprisoned in labor camps, and as part of the Great Purge, 1 million people were executed under Stalin's orders.

- **1940-1979:** Communism is established by force or otherwise in Estonia, Latvia, Lithuania, Yugoslavia, Poland, North Korea, Albania, Bulgaria, Romania, Czechoslovakia, East Germany, Hungary, China, Tibet, North Vietnam, Guinea, Cuba, Yemen, Kenya, Sudan, Congo, Burma, Angola, Benin, Cape Verde, Laos, Kampuchea, Madagascar, Mozambique, South Vietnam, Somalia, Seychelles, Afghanistan, Grenada, Nicaragua, and others.

Cold War Begins

- **May 9, 1945:** The U.S.S.R. declares victory over Nazi Germany in World War II. With

Japan's defeat, Korea becomes divided into the communist North (which the Soviets occupied) and the South (which had been occupied by the United States).

- **March 12, 1947:** President Harry S. Truman addresses Congress in what would come to be known as the Truman Doctrine, calling for the containment of communism, and later leading to the U.S. entering into wars in Vietnam and Korea to provide defense from communist takeovers. The doctrine becomes the basis for America's Cold War policy.

- **March 5, 1946:** Great Britain Prime Minister Winston Churchill makes his famous "Iron Curtain" speech in Missouri, alerting Americans to the division between the Soviet Union and the Western allies.

- **October 1, 1949:** Following a civil war, China's Communist Party leader, Mao Zedong declares his creation of the People's Republic of China, leading the United States to end diplomatic ties with the PRC for decades.

- **July 5, 1950:** Leading United Nations forces, the first U.S. troops engage in the Korean War, after communist North Korea invaded South Korea with the intent of creating a unified communist state. The war would last until July 27, 1953, with North Korea, China, and the United Nations signing an armistice agreement.

Communists Win in Cuba

- **January 1, 1959:** Fidel Castro overthrows the corrupt Fulgencio Batista regime, and Cuba becomes a communist state.

While communism is continuing its spread of influence, as noted above, the technology revolution and the advent of birth control pills start to play a major role in society, especially as we get into the 1960s. Let's temporarily turn our focus away from History.com's Communist Timeline to look at these two major worldwide societal changes.

The major invention of this time period was television, which catapulted humanity into a technology revolution. No new invention entered American homes faster than black-and-white TV sets. The TV Golden Age was between 1953 and 1955, and by 1955, half of all U.S. homes had one. In 1964, color broadcasting began on primetime TV. By the late 1960s, the content on television had started to change as well as that involving the motion picture industry.[17]

In 1968, the Motion Picture Association of America (MPAA) established a system of movie ratings for parents to use as a guide to determine the appropriateness of film content for children and teenagers. The MPAA rating system replaced the Hay's Production Code, used from the 1930s through 1966, which the U.S. Motion Picture Industry had adopted as a policy of self-censorship. The Hay's Production Code listed specifics about what would

---

[17] https://stephens.hosti ng.nyu.edu/History%20of%20Television%20page.html

not be permitted in films and a vague imperative that films should not lower the moral standard of viewers. In 1968, the Supreme Court opined that local governments could not ban movies shown to adults but could pass laws preventing children from being exposed to certain material. The norms of the 1960s allowed for more candid depictions of immoral matter and there was greater acceptance of more explicit degrees of nudity, sexuality and violence.[18]

While the 1950s and early 1960s portrayed a "father knows best" view of the family, by the 1980s, sitcoms typically portrayed the father as the family fool. Talk shows discussing subjects that were formerly taboo also became popular in the 1980s.

It is interesting as a side note that St. Elizabeth Ann Seton, the first citizen born in the United States to be given the title of "Saint," had a vision back in the mid-1800s. She indicated that she saw in the future that, "Every American would have a black box in their home through which the devil would enter."[19]

The other major factor that occurred during this time period of the 1960s and needs to be included in our discussion is the advent of the birth control pill. It was actually introduced in May of 1950 and was marketed originally for "cycle control" because contraception was taboo socially, legally and politically. In the U.S. the Comstock Law prohibited public discussion and research

---

[18] https://www.mtsu.edu/first-amendment/article/1247/motion-picture-ratings
[19] Air Waves from Hell, Review of Television, Fr. Frank Poncelet, The Neumann Press, 1991

about contraception. In 1960, in the U.S., the FDA approved oral contraception, and in Canada the pill was available for "menstrual regulation." At this point, the pill was to be prescribed exclusively for cycle control and only to married women. (Unmarried women gained access 10 years later.) In 1961, Searle obtained approval for Enovid, the first hormonal birth control pill. Within two years of its initial distribution, 1.2 million women were using oral contraception.[20]

In 1968, Pope Paul VI condemned the pill as an "artificial" means of birth control and thus sinful. The pill cleared the way for the introduction of an expanded range of hormone-based contraceptives.[21]

Every church in Christendom had condemned contraception until 1930, when, at its decennial Anglican Lambeth Conference, Anglicanism gave permission for the use of contraception in a few extraordinary cases. Soon all Protestant denominations had adopted the secularist position on contraception. Today, not one stands with the Catholic Church to maintain the ancient Christian faith on this issue.[22]

The advent of the pill was concomitant with the sexual revolution, which was so prevalent and received so much publicity, especially in the United States during the 1960s.

Thus, we can see that the 1960s brought in major widespread social changes with the television advancing

---

[20] https://journalofethics.ama-assn.org/issue/vision-and-illusion-medical-practice, https://journalofethics.ama-assn.org/sites/journalofethics.ama-assn.org/files/2020-12/joe-0006.pdf

[21] https://www.ncbi.nlm.nih.gov/pmc/articles/PMC3520685/

[22] https://www.catholic.com/magazine/print-edition/contraception

the technology revolution, as well as increased access to the birth control pill. In the meantime, communism marched on. Let's resume the Communism Timeline[23] where we left off previously:

Communists win in Vietnam

- **April 25, 1976:** Following the fall of Saigon at the end of the Vietnam War, South Vietnam's capital is seized by communist forces. A few months later, in July, the nation is reunified as the Socialist Republic of Vietnam under communist rule.
- **October 25, 1983:** The United States invades Grenada under orders of President Ronald Reagan to secure the safety of American Nationals under the country's communist regime, led by Prime Minister Maurice Bishop. The pro-Marxist government was overthrown in about a week.
- **June 4, 1989:** After weeks of protests, the communist Chinese government sends in its military to fire on demonstrators calling for democracy in Beijing's Tiananmen Square. The bloody violence ends in hundreds to thousands of deaths. (No official death toll was ever released.)

---

[23] Communism Timeline, History.com

Berlin Wall Falls, Soviet Union Dissolves

- **November 9, 1989:** The Berlin Wall, that separated communist East Berlin from democratic West Berlin for nearly 30 years, falls. The years 1989 to 1990 see the collapse of communist regimes in Czechoslovakia, Hungary, Bulgaria, Poland, Romania, Benin, Mozambique, Nicaragua and Yemen.

- **December 25, 1991:** With the resignation of Mikhail Gorbachev, the Soviet Union is dissolved. New Russian president, Boris Yeltsin bans the communist party. Communism soon ends in Afghanistan, Albania, Angola, Congo, Kenya, Yugoslavia and other nations. China, Cuba, Laos, and Vietnam remain under communist rule. North Korea remains nominally communist, although the North Korean government doesn't call itself communist.

Although communism appears to have collapsed in multiple areas of the world after the fall of the Berlin Wall, is it actually as "gone" as many people think?

There is a school of thought that the atheistic communist influence instead moved from being overt to covert, from being plainly seen to hidden. In the book *How the Specter of Communism is Ruling Our World* by The Epoch Times, the following is noted in the introduction:

The collapse of the communist regimes in the Soviet Union and Eastern Europe mark the end of a half-century-long Cold War between the capitalist and communist camps in the West and the East. At the time, many were optimistic, believing that communism had become a relic of the past.

The sad truth, however, is that a transmogrified communist ideology has taken hold and entrenched itself around the world. In China, North Korea, Cuba and Vietnam, there are outright communist regimes; in Eastern European countries, communist ideology and customs still exert a significant influence; and in African and South American countries, socialism is practiced under the banner of democracy and republicanism. Then there are the nations of Western Europe and North America which have become host to communist influences without people even realizing it.[24]

Within the west there is the thought that communism just underwent a more socially acceptable transformation and from it came the spread of secularism, atheism and materialism, with a decline in the traditional moral and cultural beliefs. This brought with it a backlash against the traditional family with an emphasis on sexual immorality. And while technology was simultaneously further advancing, it meant that these ideas could be easily and quickly spread around the world.

With further time and the advent of the Internet, information could be exchanged essentially instantly. As a tool, this has potential for tremendous good but also tremendous misuse. On the side of good, stories of the lives of the saints, prayers, and catholic websites can be

---

[24] *How the Specter of Communism is Ruling Our World* by The Epoch Times, copyright 2020.

of immense help to the faithful, with information and opportunities for evangelization. The ability to easily communicate over time and distance for business/pleasure or with other likeminded faith-filled people is also a tremendous benefit. And while the technological advances do have their definite pros, there are also significant cons that have been noted. Just a few of these include internet addiction, online gaming addiction, damage to social relationships with social isolation, malicious online behavior, viewing online pornography, impairment of private and public boundaries, and even harmful effects on cognitive development.

So we can see from our brief walk-through recent history that many changes have occurred in our world with various ramifications. Where has it all taken us? And since this is a book with a Catholic emphasis, what about from the faith perspective? How did the Catholic church fare during this time period? What happened to Catholic faith and belief?

Well, in answering those specific questions regarding the Catholic faith, the results are definitely suboptimal; from the perspective of the Catholic church, the statistics of this historical period are not kind. While there has been growth of the church in Africa during this time period, the numbers in the west have shown a significant decline. Data from the Center for Applied Research in the Apostolate reveals staggering results. The following U.S. data shows the changes that occurred between 1970 and 2021:

- A decrease in total priests from 59,192 to 34,923

- Religious sisters decreased from 160,931 to 39,452
- Religious brothers decreased from 11,623 to 3,832
- Parishes without a resident priest pastor increased from 571 to 3,377

During this time, the Catholic population actually increased from 54.1 million to 73.2 million, largely due to an increase in foreign-born adult Catholics (an increase from negligible/not counted to 14.9 million). Unfortunately though, during this same time frame, former Catholic adults, i.e. those raised Catholic who no longer self-identify as Catholic, increased from 3.5 million to 30.8 million.[25] This is almost a nine times increase in formerly-Catholic adults!

As far as religious education, sacraments, and Mass attendance go, during the same time frame from 1970 to 2021:

- Students in Catholic elementary schools decreased from 3.4 million to 1.1 million.
- Students in Catholic secondary schools decreased from 1.008 million to 535,844.
- Baptisms of infants in the previous year declined from 1.089 million to 411,482.
- Marriages in the previous year decreased from 426,309 to 97,200.

---

[25] Center for Applied Research in the Apostolate, 2300 Wisconsin Avenue Northwest, Ste 400A, Washington, DC 20007, United States (Data based on survey-based estimates.)

- Catholics who attend Mass every week declined from 54.9% to 17.3%.

Another survey that was done by the Center for Applied Research in the Apostolate regarding Catholic young adults indicated that 13% of Catholic young adults attended Mass at least once a week before the COVID 19 pandemic. The study indicated, "perhaps of greater concern to the church, 73% agreed 'somewhat' or 'strongly' that they could be a good Catholic without going to Mass every Sunday. Only 39% agreed 'somewhat' or 'strongly' that they could never imagine themselves leaving the Catholic Church."

The statistics are even more concerning when looking at parts of Western Europe. In France, for instance, in the early 1960s, 96% of French people indicated they were baptized Catholics. According to the 2018 "European Values Survey," only 32% of French people now identify as Catholics, of whom less than 5% attend weekly Mass.

The figures are noted to be even worse for young people in France. Another 2018 study, "Europe's Young Adults and Religion" found that only 23% of French people ages 16-29 identify as Catholics, 7% of whom attend weekly Mass. "All told, a barrel bottom scraping 1.61% of French people in this age group attend weekly Mass."[26]

Further devastating the overall picture is the clerical sexual abuse crisis. Even a single victimization by a shepherd of God is an unspeakable tragedy. But in addition to this, and from a wider perspective, there has

---

[26] New Oxford Review, January/February 2022, page 30, 31

been an overall decline of moral standards associated with the Church. Even with the actual number of priest abusers being a minority, it still hurts those many good priests who are actually serving God. For instance, these good priests who are faithful to Catholic teaching must be very careful in their everyday dealings with people. Accusations can occur with little to no validity by those who oppose the priest (or at least the faithful teachings he stands for). The Church has tarnished her reputation with the sexual abuse crisis and thus decreased her credibility, especially when dealing with the greater moral issues of our day. Personally, I have two nephews who are priests. They are people just like everyone else and benefit from our appreciation, support and prayers.

We began this chapter looking at the historical context of the movement of Freemasonry and of the timeline of Russia with the growth of communism. We also included basic technologic advances (television) and societal issues of the 1960s (the birth control pill) which contributed. We noted at the end of the chapter that the Catholic church did not statistically fare well during this time period. We have covered a history of various events with many myriad topics. So how do we pull all of these things together? Where do we go from here?

In the following chapter, we will look at how the events contained in this chapter appear through the eyes of the Blessed Mother. We will do this by looking at the approved Marian apparitions that are applicable within this same historical context. As we shall see, her view will give us some illumination and insight.

Chapter 4

A Mother's View

Human history at its core is based on human thought and action. It is a series of events including what, when, where, how and by whom. The why can sometimes be a little more complicated, however. There is another way of looking at human history, though, that goes deep below the surface. With the eyes of faith, another perspective on what caused this human thought and action is possible. It is a level of reality not immediately available to the strict materialist, a spiritual level which in actuality can underpin the ongoing human decisions and interactions of the material world.

Let's look at the events we discussed in the last chapter through the eyes of faith, more specifically, the eyes of the Blessed Virgin Mary. We can do this via the approved apparitions which occurred during this same time span.

Our Lady of Guadalupe in 1531 was the first formally approved Marian apparition. (See Appendix 2 for a summary of the apparition.) It resulted in millions of conversions at the time, and the miraculous imprint of the image of the Virgin on the tilma still gives us pause today. The fact that the image is of a pregnant woman made it not only pertinent to the human sacrificing that was going on at the time, but also to the tragedy of abortion which is going on in our own day and age. While there are not specific predictions for our times, the pro-life theme and multiple miracles involving the tilma itself continue to give a strong message.

The next approved Marian apparition which is even more strongly predictive of our current era is Our Lady of Good Success in Quito, Ecuador beginning in the year 1594. (See Appendix 3 for a summary of the apparition.) As God utilized prophets hundreds of years in advance in the Old Testament, so this prophet, visionary and convent foundress Mother Mariana, was utilized hundreds of years in advance with messages for our current era. She was told of a time of a great falling away from the church, a time of total corruption of customs, and that Satan would reign almost completely by the means of the masonic sects. She noted that "unbridled luxury" would "ensnare" people into sin and cause "innumerable frivolous souls who will be lost." She foretold the priest scandal, how the sacrament of matrimony would be attacked and profaned, and how the Catholic spirit would rapidly decay. She talked about the assault on childhood innocence and how the "spirit of impurity will saturate the atmosphere of those times. Like a filthy ocean, it will run through the streets, squares and public places within an astonishing liberty."

Mother Mariana was given an apparition on a Good Friday when she was actually shown the horrible abuses and heresies that would exist in the church in our times. She was noted to actually die after seeing this apparition until she was resurrected two days later on Easter Sunday morning. This mystical, and yet physical phenomenon was an extraordinary event in her life. She further suffered voluntarily as a victim in expiation for the sins of an era hundreds of years in the future — *our* era. She had multiple miracles and signs associated with her apparitions with an exclamation mark being the fact that hundreds of years later (1906), not only herself but three other convent founding mothers in Quito, Ecuador were all found to be incorrupt![27]

The Blessed Mother as Our Lady of Good Success indicated through Mother Mariana that this era would occur, "from the end of the 19th century and from shortly after the middle of the 20th century." She also noted that "as these heresies spread and dominate the precious light of faith will be extinguished in souls by the almost total corruption of customs."

One interesting question regarding this is why does she specifically point out both at the end of the 19th century and from shortly after the middle of the 20th century as the period that Satan would reign? The middle of the 20th century is obviously after the end of the 19th century. Why doesn't she just say after the end of the 19th century rather than also pointing out after the middle of the 20th century?

To answer this question, I would propose that the Blessed Mother knew that different additive events would be occurring at the end of the 19th century versus the middle of the 20th century and thus specifically included this distinction. The first event to include is that the devil would be gradually given more power for this

---

[27] The Story of Our Lady of Good Success and Novena, Rev. Father Manuel Sousa Pereira, 2013, Dolorosa Press, Camillus, New York

era starting around the end of the 19th century. This was indeed foretold by the Virgin Mary through her apparition as Our Lady of La Salette (see Appendix 4) when in 1846 she indicated that the devil would be gradually increasing in power starting in 1864. (As an aside from our last chapter let us remember that between 1846 and 1864 is the year 1848 – the year *The Communist Manifesto* was published).

Our Lady of La Salette, in 1846, indicated the following to the visionary, Melanie:

> In the year 1864, Lucifer together with a large number of demons will be unloosed from hell; they will put an end to faith little by little, even in those dedicated to God. They will blind them in such a way, that unless they are blessed with a special grace, these people will take on the spirit of these angels in hell… Evil books will be abundant on earth, and the spirit of darkness will spread everywhere, a universal slackening in all that concerns the service of God… The vicar of my Son will have much to suffer, as, for a time, the Church will be the victim of great prosecution: this will be a time of darkness. The Church will suffer a terrible crisis.

The unleashing by the devil during this timeframe is further supported by the vision of Pope Leo XIII previously referred to in the introduction (see Appendix 11). Pope Leo XIII is well documented to have had a vision sometime between January 1884 and August 1886. It is this same Pope Leo XIII, who we discussed in the previous chapter, who had such strong condemnations of the Masonic sect. While we don't know exactly what the vision entailed, we know that it affected him so much that he composed the now commonly known St. Michael Prayer to defend against the devil. He then had this prayer of protection promulgated in the Church throughout the whole world.

So the first event as told by Our Lady of Good Success referenced the end of the 19th century and appears to be the initial unloosing of the devil into our era. If this is true, then what is the second event she included regarding "after the middle of the 20th century"?

The answer to this could be related to her further referencing the heresies spreading and dominating throughout the world. This would have only been made possible with the advent of the television and subsequent technological advances. First came the unloosening of the devil and later comes the spreading of his lies utilizing the technological advancements of the era. Thus it would make sense that the Blessed Virgin Mary would utilize two references of time including the end of the 19th century when this dark period would begin, and after the middle of the 20th century when the evil influence would really spread and dominate, thus resulting in the extensive and widespread corruption of customs as predicted.

Furthermore, Our Lady of Fatima, which occurred in 1917 (see Appendix 5), gives us even more insight as to how the heresies developed and how the corruption spread. On July 13, 1917, Our Lady told the children in Fatima:

> If people attend to my request, Russia will be converted and the world will have peace. If not, she (Russia) will scatter her errors throughout the

world, provoking wars and persecutions of the Church. The good will be martyred. The Holy Father will have much to suffer and various nations will be destroyed. ...

Now Russia, at that period of history, would not have been considered a nation of international significance. Yet in hindsight, we know that in November, of that exact same year of 1917, the Bolshevik Revolution took place. The atheistic heresies which were the foundation of Freemasonry also formed the foundation of Communism. And with the Bolshevik Revolution the growth and spreading of these Communist errors against God and the Church began.

It was 12 years later, in 1929, that Our Lady of Fatima actually asked for the consecration of Russia to her Immaculate Heart (Note: In this context the meaning of consecration is the formal act of the pope performing a dedication to God, or in this case to Mary's Immaculate Heart). She indicated to the visionary Lucia in a private message, "The moment has come in which God asks the Holy Father, in union with all the bishops of the world, to make the consecration of Russia to my Immaculate Heart, promising to save it by these means."

Unfortunately, the consecration did not take place soon after as requested and the latency did not go unnoticed by heaven above. By August 1931, in a private vision to Lucia, Our Lord indicated that the die had already been cast:

> They did not wish to heed my request. Like the King of France they will regret it and then do it, but it will be late. Russia will have already spread

her errors throughout the world, provoking wars and persecutions against the church. The Holy Father will have much to suffer.

Sure enough, in hindsight we can see the errors of Russia with atheistic communism being spread throughout the world. And as noted in the last chapter, these errors have not only been overtly involving nations that are openly communist but also covertly with the spirit of decline in the traditional moral and cultural beliefs in the west.

Nevertheless, as the loving Mother which Our Lady is, she continued to come to visit her children. With Our Lady of Akita (see Appendix 6), a statue of Our Lady began bleeding in 1973 and did not stop until 1981. Per Sister Agnes Sasagawa, who received the messages of Our Lady of Akita, her guardian angel noted that, "The blood shed by Mary has a profound meaning… To ask your conversion, to ask for peace in reparation for the ingratitude and outrages against the Lord…" The August 13, 1973 vision by Our Lady of Akita indicated that, "In order that the world might know His anger, the Heavenly Father is preparing to inflict a great chastisement on all mankind…" She indicated that, "prayer, penance and courageous sacrifices can soften the Father's anger."

In 1980 Our Lady appeared in Nicaragua as Our Lady of Cuapa (see Appendix 8), where she told the visionary Bernardo Martinez to "Pray, pray my son, the Rosary for all the world. Tell believers and non-believers that the world is threatened by grave dangers. I asked the Lord to appease His justice, but if you don't change you will hasten the arrival of the Third World War."

In 1982 in Kibeho, Africa, Our Lady as "Mother of the Word" (see Appendix 9) told visionary Marie-Claire,

> I am concerned with and turning to the whole world. The world is evil and rushes towards its ruin. It is about to fall in its abyss. The world is in rebellion against God. Many sins are being committed. There is no love and no peace. If you do not repent and convert your hearts, you will all fall into an abyss.

In 1989 in San Nicolas, Argentina, Our Lady of the Rosary (see Appendix 10) told visionary Gladys Quiroga de Motta,

> …many children in these moments are submerged in their own materialistic world and will continue so, because they do not seek the aid their spirits need in God. They all have the possibility to receive it but many reject it… Today the devil is dazzling the world so belittled in Christian spirit. The truth of Christ, that truth that is proclaimed through His mother, must reign in hearts… Give thanks to the Lord, because only He will save the people.

In 1989 in Betania, Venezuela, Our Lady as "Reconciler of People and Nations" (see Appendix 7) told visionary Maria Esperanza (along with her divine Son), "…in these times of great calamity for mankind, we are calling all Our scattered children from different places of the world to receive Our message." She also noted in 1990,

> …for great events and painful riots are growing around the world; countries and nations are being

shaken by bad times…Men have lessened their potential in regar d to their spirituality… behold they are navigating against the divine current of peace, love and brotherly unity.

So we can see messages from Our Lady from literally all over the world sharing her concerns and guiding us. She is calling us to conversion, to focus on our faith.

In the end of our last chapter we discussed the effect of these current times on the Catholic church. We reviewed some recent statistics which unfortunately revealed a significant loss of faith, especially in the west. In addition, we noted the priest abuse scandal. These events were also foretold by Our Lady. In fact, Our Lady of Good Success prophesied back in 1611 that during our era,

> The sacred sacrament of Holy Orders will be ridiculed, oppressed and despised… The devil will try to persecute the ministers of the Lord in every possible way. He will labor with cool and subtle astuteness to deviate them from the spirit of their vocation and will corrupt many of them. These depraved priests who will scandalize the Christian people will make the hatred of the bad Catholics and the enemies of the Roman Catholic and apostolic church fall upon all priests. This apparent triumph of Satan will bring enormous suffering upon the good pastors of the church….

Our Lady of Good Success does not stop there. She continues,

> Further, in these unhappy times, there will be unbridled luxury which will ensnare the rest into sin and conquer innumerable frivolous souls who will be lost. Innocence will almost no longer be found in children, nor modesty in women. In this supreme moment of need of the church, the one who should speak will fall silent… During these unfortunate times evil will assault childhood innocence. In this way, vocations to the priesthood will be lost which will be a true calamity.

She also foretold of the marked decline in the number of Catholic nuns; "There will be almost no virgin souls in the world."

Our Lady of Good Success continued,

> During this epic, the Church will herself be attacked by terrible hoards of the Masonic sect …" and that there would be, "…agonizing because of the corruption of customs, unbridled luxury and extravagance, the impious press and secular education. The vices of impurity, blasphemy, and sacrilege will dominate in this time of depraved desolation…

These statements were a prelude to similar statements from Our Lady of La Salette who in 1846 foretold the devastating loss of faith that has now occurred in France. In a message to visionary Maximin Giraud, Our Lady of La Salette predicted, "France has corrupted the universe, one day it will be punished. The faith will die out in France, three quarters of France will not practice religion anymore, or almost no more, the other part will practice it without really practicing it." Our Lady of La Salette also told the other visionary, Melanie Giraud, "All the civil governments will have one and the same plan, which will be to abolish and do away with every religious principle, to make way for materialism, atheism, spiritualism and vices of all kinds."

This same theme was continued at Fatima in Portugal with subsequent messages to the young visionary Jacinta before her death in 1920:

- "The sins of the world are very great. … If men only knew what eternity is, they would do everything in their power to change their lives."… "You must pray much for sinners and priests and religious."
- "Priests must be pure, very pure. They should not busy themselves with anything except what concerns the Church and souls…"
- "Fly from riches and luxury; love poverty and silence; have charity even for bad people."
- "More souls go to Hell because of sins of the flesh than for any other reason."
- "Certain fashions will be introduced that will offend Our Lord very much."
- "The Mother of God wants more virgin souls bound by the vow of chastity."
- "Woe to women wanting in modesty."
- "Let men avoid greed, lies, envy, blasphemy, impurity."

We are also reminded of the messages of Our Lady of Akita:

- "Pray very much for the pope, bishops and priests…."
- "The work of the devil will infiltrate even into the Church in such a way that one will see cardinals opposing cardinals, bishops against bishops. The priests who venerate me will be scorned and opposed by their confreres… churches and altars sacked, the Church will be full of those who accept compromises and the demon will press many priests and consecrated souls to leave the service of the Lord."
- "The demon will be especially implacable against souls consecrated to God. The thought of the loss of so many souls is the cause of my sadness. If sins increase in number and gravity, there will be no longer pardon for them."

In summarizing this chapter, we can see that the prophecies of Our Lady, from literally all over the world, appear true and are definitely applicable to our times. We can gain a greater understanding of the historical context when illuminated by her messages and insights. We can also see from the above that the Catholic Church (especially in the west) has indeed suffered greatly during these times.

So where is all of this taking us? What lies ahead in the future? Is the world coming to an end? Or is it the end of an era? What does Our Lady have to say? Let's look more closely at these questions in the next chapter.

Chapter 5

THE END OF THE WORLD OR THE END OF AN ERA?

I grew up in a small city in the U.S.A. (Winona, MN, population 25,000), in a middle-class neighborhood in the 1960s and 1970s. I remember when I was 5 years old, I learned how to ride a bike and rode all over the neighborhood with the other neighborhood kids. There was no concern regarding child abduction. It was unthinkable. Society was in the midst of the baby boom movement. Our phone number was four digits long and we shared a "party line" with other people who might also be on the line, and thus you had to wait your turn. This was before we even obtained a black-and-white television, which occurred later on in the 1960s. No one locked their doors in the neighborhood. Why would you do that? The first burglary in the late 1960s sent shockwaves through the local community. The vestiges of the Christian foundation of our country were still very much present. Most neighbors either went to Catholic Mass or Protestant services on Sunday. Most stores were closed on Sunday, save some gas stations and restaurants. There was still a certain innocence, a respect for others, a modesty and faithfulness to the God above which permeated the culture of that time.

Unfortunately, we have seen a marked moral decline in society since that period. Certainly technological advancement has had its role in spreading this, but technology is simply a tool which can be used either for good or bad. It was this spirit of kindness, respect, modesty and faithfulness to God, as noted above, that appears to have been markedly weakened. I am reminded of a trip that I took to a large European city several years back. While on a city bus, there plastered across from me, was a large advertising poster of a woman essentially unclothed. As I tried to guard my eyes, I looked up to the top of the bus and there were similar ones there! I then averted my eyes to some of the people who were riding on the bus, which revealed several women who were immodestly dressed. Finally my eyes rested down on the floor, where I looked at my feet until arriving at the destination. As Our Lady said with her prophesies from Our Lady of Good Success, "…the spirit of impurity will saturate the atmosphere in those times. Like a filthy ocean, it will run through the streets, squares and public places with an astonishing liberty."

So where will this downward moral slide take us? After all, Our Lady of Akita discusses a great chastisement and fire from the sky. Our Lady of Cuapa references a third world war. What is coming before us? Is it Armageddon? Is Jesus' second coming on the horizon?

Many of our Protestant brethren hold a belief in the rapture; that when times get difficult, Christ will take them out of the ever-increasing discord in the world. They will rise "in the clouds, to meet with the Lord in the air" (1 Thessalonians 4:17). This is a huge movement, fueled in part by the *Left Behind* series,[28] which was enormously popular and spawned multiple books and movies. Yet for those who are caught up in the whole rapture belief system, there is an amount of emotional trauma that's lately been documented. The term "rapture anxiety" has been coined for the emotional trauma of those who have continued to essentially be on edge, thinking they are going to be raptured at any time, and also coming to terms with the fact that it hasn't happened yet. While belief in the rapture is not part of our Catholic faith, there is nevertheless concern for our Protestant brothers and sisters and compassion for the emotional trauma and suffering these Christian groups have experienced.

And while we are discussing these Protestant Christian apocalyptic beliefs, what about other pagan/worldly influences in this regard? What about the Y2K debacle at the turn of the century that was supposed to totally turn the world upside down? Or the 2012 phenomenon which was predicated by the Mayan calendar?

So what is the truth? Is the world going to end? And is it soon? Since we have been focusing on Our Lady's approved messages, let's take a look at what she has to say about the topic.

Hundreds of years ago, in the early 1600s, Our Lady of Good Success indicated that our current era would first include a time of increased evil influence and then be followed by her triumph. She noted that when this evil influence will seem to be at its worst, "This, then, will

---

[28] Tim LaHaye, Jerry B. Jenkins, Tyndale House Publishers 1995

mark the arrival of my hour when I in a marvelous way will dethrone the proud and cursed Satan, trampling him under my feet and fettering him in the infernal abyss." She further prophesied, "To test this faith and confidence of the just, there will be occasions when everything will seem to be lost and paralyzed. This will be, then, the happy beginning of the complete restoration."

She asked for us to pray to God, our Father, to bring an end to these ominous times:

> Therefore, pray insistently without tiring and weep with bitter tears in the secrecy of your heart. Implore our celestial Father that for love of the Eucharistic Heart of my most Holy Son and His precious blood shed with such generosity ... He might take pity on His ministers and bring to an end those ominous times…

So Our Lady of Good Success talks about this new era as the "arrival of my hour" and a "complete restoration" that will "bring an end to these ominous times."

But this is not the only Marian apparition which discusses a coming era of triumph and change. Our Lady of La Salette is even more detailed in her predictions of an era of peace that is to come. The La Salette visionary Maximin Giraud was only 11 years old when he saw the Blessed Mother in 1846. This is his accounting of what Our Lady said:

> …great disorders will arrive, in the Church, and everywhere. Then, after that, our Holy Father the Pope will be persecuted. His successor will be a pontiff that nobody expects. Then, after that, a

> great peace will come, but it will not last a long time. A monster will come to disturb it.

This quote references a coming era of peace but describes it as short-lived. The allusion to a monster is interesting and would appear to indicate the actual person of the Antichrist coming at the end of the upcoming era of peace. (This is not unique thinking as there is a history of Catholic prophetic thought from the Middle Ages that also refers to this future sequence of events, i.e. after an increased time of trial on earth there is a time of peace, and after the time of peace is the coming of the actual person of the Antichrist, which is then followed by the second coming of Christ.)

The other La Salette visionary, Melanie Giraud, accounts from Our Lady:

> The righteous will suffer greatly. Their prayers, their penance and their tears will rise up to Heaven, and all of God's people will beg for forgiveness and mercy and will plead for my help and intercession. And then Jesus Christ, in an act of His justice and His great mercy will command His angels to have all His enemies put to death. Suddenly, the persecutors of the Church of Jesus Christ and all those given over to sin will perish and the earth will be desert-like. And then peace will be made, and man will be reconciled with God. Jesus Christ will be served, worshiped and glorified. Charity will flourish everywhere. The new kings will be the right arm of the Holy Church, which will be strong, humble, pious in its poor but fervent imitations of Jesus Christ.

> The Gospel will be preached everywhere and mankind will make great progress in its Faith, for there will be unity among the workers of Jesus Christ and man will live in fear of God.

Melanie also noted the following regarding the coming era of peace: "This peace among men will be short-lived. Twenty-five years of plentiful harvest will make them forget that the sins of men are the cause of all the troubles on this earth."

Our Lady of La Salette not only gives us information of what this coming era of peace will entail, but also tells us how long it will last.

Lastly, Our Lady of Fatima also talks about a period of peace. The following is from her July 13, 1917, message to the children, "In the end, my Immaculate Heart will triumph. The Holy Father will consecrate Russia to me. It will be converted and a certain period of peace will be granted to the world." With Our Lady of Fatima, however, this issue of a "period of peace" is quite intriguing as it can also be noted as a past event. This will be covered further in the next chapter.

So in summary, we recall that the question we started this chapter with was whether we are nearing the end of the world or the end of an era. As we can see from both Our Lady of Good Success and Our Lady of La Salette, it is apparent that the answer is the end of an era rather than the end of the world. Our Lady of Good Success talks about a coming peaceful era as the "arrival of my hour" and a "complete restoration" that will "bring an end to these ominous times." She implores us to pray to shorten these ongoing times of trial so that this time of peace and restoration can come even sooner. Our Lady of La Salette further describes what is involved in this period of peace, noting that "Charity will flourish everywhere," and she actually gives us a prediction of how long it will last.

Our Lady of Fatima also predicted that in the end her Immaculate Heart would triumph and that a certain period of peace will be granted to the world. We will look more closely at Our Lady of Fatima and this topic in the next chapter.

CHAPTER 6

DID THE PERIOD OF PEACE FORETOLD AT FATIMA ALREADY HAPPEN?

It is during the July 13, 1917 vision that the children are told by Our Lady of Fatima that she will come to ask for the consecration of Russia to her Immaculate Heart and makes reference to a period of peace:

> If my requests are heeded, Russia will be converted and there will be peace; if not, she will spread her errors throughout the world causing wars and persecutions of the church. The good will be martyred; the Holy Father will have much to suffer, various nations will be annihilated. In the end my Immaculate Heart will triumph. The Holy Father will consecrate Russia to me and she shall be converted and a period of peace will be granted to the world.

Twelve years later, on June 13, 1929, the remaining living Fatima seer Lucia received an additional vision from the Blessed Virgin Mary at Tuy, Spain indicating that the time for requesting the consecration had come. Our Lady indicated to Lucia:

The moment has come in which God asks the Holy Father, in union with all the bishops of the world, to make the consecration of Russia to my Immaculate Heart, promising to save it by this means. There are so many souls whom the justice of God condemns for sins committed against me, that I have come to ask reparation: sacrifice yourself for this intention and pray.

The momentum within the greater Church regarding Fatima was building and on October 13, 1930 the apparitions were officially approved. Unfortunately, the consecration was not done during this initial timeframe as was requested, and Lucia received a follow up vision, this time by our Lord in 1931 at Rianjo, Spain. During this vision Jesus told her:

> …Make it known to My ministers, that given they follow the example of the King of France in delaying the execution of My request, that they will follow him into misfortune. Like the King of France, they will repent and will do as I have requested, but it will be very late: Russia will already have spread her errors throughout the world, causing wars and persecutions against the Church. The Holy Father will have much to suffer! But it will never be too late to have recourse to Jesus and Mary.

So we see in the above quote regarding the consecration of Russia, that our Lord indicates that it will be done, but that it will be done very late. He notes that Russia will have already spread her errors throughout the world. He also references the King of France and makes a similarity to the Holy Father. This reference of our Lord to the King of France is very important for our ongoing discussions.

Back in the late 1600s, King Louis XIV of France was at that time the greatest monarch in Europe and ruled from his palace in Versailles. On June 17, 1689, Our Lord manifested as the Sacred Heart of Jesus to a French nun, Saint Margaret Mary Alacoque. Through her, his command to the King of France was that the King was to consecrate himself and France to the Sacred Heart of Jesus. This manifestation happened one year before the holy demise of St. Margaret Mary at the age of 43. The following is this command to King Louis XIV by Our Lord through St. Margaret Mary Alacoque:

> Make it known to the eldest son of My Sacred Heart, that as his temporal birth was obtained by devotion to the merits of My Holy Childhood, so he will get his birth to eternal glory by the consecration which he will make of himself to My Adorable Heart, which means his triumph, and through it, to the great of the earth. I want My Heart to reign in his palace, to be painted on his standard and engraved in his arms, to make him victorious over all his enemies, and by placing at his feet these proud foes, to make him victorious over all enemies of the Holy Church.

This request was sent to the king's confessor to no avail. Finally, in that same year, St. Margaret Mary went to Versailles to seek King Louis XIV. France at that time had never seemed more glorious and was on the cusp of innovating its culture, technology and industry. It had the highest population in Europe (therefore the largest armies), and was undefeated on the battlefield.

Unfortunately the "Rois-Soleil" or "Sun King" flat out refused the request from heaven. King Louis XIV never attended to our Lord's request, nor did his son, King Louis XV, nor initially even his grandson, King Louis XVI. For 100 years the Kings of France delayed and did not obey. Meanwhile, as time went by, the people were getting increasingly disgusted with the French aristocracy and the royal economic policies and the foundations for the French Revolution were underway. Exactly 100 years later to the day (June 17, 1789), the grandson and then current King of France, King Louis XVI was stripped of his authority. He was placed on house arrest with the sights and sounds of revolution steadily growing around him. It was only in this environment that King Louis XVI made the pious consecration of both himself and his country to the Sacred Heart of Jesus. It was a very thorough consecration to the Sacred Heart of Jesus[29] (see Appendix 12), but unfortunately, it was too late. The French Revolution was continuing to gain momentum, and four years later in 1793 he was executed at the guillotine.[30]

However, it would not be just France that would inherit the misfortune of King Louis XVI, but the rest of Europe and beyond. It is more than interesting to note

---

[29] Consecration of Louis XVI, King of France, to the Sacred Heart of Jesus, https://nobility.org/2017/07/consecration-louis-xvi-france-sacred-heart/

[30] My dear France, the tender daughter of the Sacred Heart No.3, Dr. Edouard Belaga, Catholicstand.com

that the so called "Enlightenment" period, generally known to have occurred from the 1690s to the 1790s, followed very closely to the same 100-year period of the initial request for the consecration of France to the French Revolution.[31]

Central to the Enlightenment agenda was the assault on what they held as "religious superstition" and its replacement by rational religion, which is most commonly referred to as Deism. Deism is a heresy which holds that God became no more than the supreme intelligence or craftsman who had set the machine that was the world to run according to its own natural and predictable laws. In other words, God made the world and then left it. In accordance with Deism is the belief that the supernatural world of miracles and much of the Bible is false. It was thus during this period that many people beginning in Europe began to question Christian concepts and morality.

This reference of Our Lord in 1931 to Lucia regarding the analogy of the King of France was thus in and of itself ominous. Things obviously did not end well with the King of France and the concern was that history would repeat itself. At that time, Our Lord indicated a future where the consecration requested at Fatima to the Immaculate Heart would be very late and that Russia would have already spread her errors throughout the world.

Sister Lucia was obviously concerned with this distressing prophesy. Time was passing and still no papal consecration was being done. In May 1936, she asked

---

[31] Timeline of the Enlightenment, history teacher.net

Our Lord why he did not want to convert Russia without the Holy Father making the consecration. Jesus replied,

> Because I want my whole church to acknowledge the consecration as a triumph of the Immaculate Heart of Mary, so that it may extend its cult later, and put the devotion to my mother's Immaculate Heart aside the devotion to my Sacred Heart.

Sister Lucia exclaimed, "But the Holy Father will never believe me, Lord, unless you, yourself move him with a special inspiration." He replied, "The Holy Father! Pray very much for the Holy Father. He will do the consecration but it will be very late! Nevertheless, the Immaculate Heart of Mary will save Russia which has been entrusted to her."

In a likewise manner, Our Lord told Sister Lucia in 1940 when Europe was engaged in World War II:

> Pray for the Holy Father; sacrifice yourself so that his heart will not succumb to the bitterness that oppresses him. The persecutions will increase; I will punish the nations with war and famine: the persecution against my church will weigh heavily upon my vicar on earth. His Holiness will be able to shorten these times of tribulation if he fulfils my desire of consecrating the whole world, and of Russia in particular, to the Immaculate Heart of Mary.

While Word War II was thus continuing to rage, Pope Pius XII performed a consecration which was done on October 31, 1942. He consecrated the world to the Immaculate Heart of Mary, but without doing it quite as

Our Lord had requested. In response Sister Lucia declared the following,

> Our Lord has accepted the consecration of the world of October 1942, to the Immaculate Heart of Mary, and promises to put a rapid end to the war. Furthermore, as the consecration was not done fully as he requested, the conversion of Russia will not take place for now."

World War II ended in 1945. In 1946, in an interview with the writer, William Thomas Walsh, Sister Lucia declared:

> What Our Lady wants is for the Holy Father and all the bishops to consecrate Russia to her Immaculate Heart, in a special ceremony. If this consecration is made, the Blessed Virgin will convert Russia and peace will reign in the world. Otherwise, Russia will spread her errors throughout the world.

In 1952, the Blessed Virgin told Sister Lucia, "Make it known to the Holy Father that I continue to wait for the consecration of Russia to my Immaculate Heart. Without this consecration, Russia will not convert and the world will not enjoy peace."

It was thus in that same year, 1952, Pope Pius XII consecrated "The peoples of Russia, specifically" although he did not perform this act in union with the bishops of the world. Pope Paul VI renewed the partial consecration during the Cold War period in 1964.

On May 13, 1981, the Feast of Our Lady of Fatima, in St. Peter's Square in Vatican City, Pope John Paul II was shot twice and wounded in an attempted assassination. After his subsequent recovery, he traveled to Fatima and on May 13, 1982, which was the first anniversary of the attempt on his life, he made an act of consecration of the "world" to Our Lady. Unfortunately, it was not done with all of the bishops of the world and thus Sister Lucia said that the consecration did not fulfill the necessary conditions. It was later in that same year when Sister Lucia wrote to Pope John Paul II:

> Since we did not heed this appeal of the message, we see that it has been fulfilled. Russia has invaded the world with her errors, and if we have not yet seen the complete fulfillment of the final part of this prophesy, we are going towards it, little by little, with great strides if we do not reject the path of sin, hatred, revenge, injustice, violations of the rights of the human person, immorality and violence, etc.
>
> And let us not say that it is God who is punishing us in this way; on the contrary it is people themselves who are preparing their own punishment. In his kindness, God warns us and calls us to the right path, while respecting the freedom he has given us; hence people are responsible.[32]

Thus in 1984, Pope John Paul II repeated the consecration which in part reads as follows:

---

[32] Visionary Sister Lucia in a letter to the Holy Father May 12, 1982, "The Message of Fatima" Vatican.va

The Coming Era of Peace

> In a special way, we entrust and consecrate to you those individuals and nations which particularly need to be thus entrusted and consecrated. We have recourse to your protection Holy Mother of God! Despise not our petitions in our necessities.[33]

As Pope John Paul II had written to the bishops of the world and asked them to join him for this public consecration, it was later noted by Sister Lucia to have been accepted as requested. Sister Lucia noted in a personal handwritten letter,

> Supreme Pontiff, John Paul II, wrote to all the bishops of the world asking them to unite with him. He sent for the statue of Our Lady of Fatima – the one from the little chapel to be taken to Rome and on March 25, 1984 – publicly – with the bishops who wanted to unite with His Holiness, made the consecration as Our Lady requested. They then asked me if it was made as Our Lady requested, and I said 'Yes.' Now it was made.[34]

Sister Lucia also said in a 1990 letter to Fr. Robert J. Fox: "Yes, it was accomplished, and since then I have said that it was made. And I say that no other person responds for me, it is I who receive and open all letters and respond to them.[35]

It was on November 9, 1989, that the Berlin wall came down and on December 26, 1991, that the Soviet

---

[33] Pope John Paul II, the Message of Fatima, Vatican.va
[34] Letter to St. Mary of Bethlehem, Coimbra, August 29, 1989
[35] Coimbra, July 3, 1990, Sister Lucia

Union dissolved thus ending the Cold War. This, of course, was a momentous occasion and occurred without a single shot being fired. The "period of peace" which was prophesied at Fatima had begun.

This ends the story, right? Or does it? As it turns out, with the passing of time there has been more and more controversy regarding this. If there is now peace in the world, some have asked, where it is located? It could be noted that not long after the crumbling of the Soviet Bloc there were episodes of genocide in Rwanda, human trafficking rings in Bosnia, the purging of Christians from the Middle East, and ongoing abortions in many countries.

There were those who questioned whether Sister Lucia had simply gotten caught up in the moment with the collapsing of the Soviet Union after the consecration. Included in this group was Fr. David Francisquini, who said in the Brazilian magazine *Revista Catolicismo* in 2020:

> It is legitimate to conjecture that, when re-evaluating the act of John Paul II in 1984, Sister Lucia allowed herself to be influenced by the atmosphere of optimism that spread in the world after the collapse of the Soviet empire. It should be noted that Sister Lucia did not enjoy the charism of infallibility in the interpretation of the lofty messages she received. Therefore, it is for the church's historians, theologians, and pastors to analyze the consistency of these statements, collected by Cardinal Bertone, with the previous statements of Sister Lucia herself. However, one thing is clear: the fruits of the consecration of

Russia to the Immaculate of Heart of Mary, announced by Our Lady, are far from having materialized. There is no peace in the world.[36]

Cardinal Raymond Burke, in a speech in 2017, when commenting about the "de-Christianization in our day" and our "completely secularized society" asked for a reconsecration of Russia to the Immaculate Heart:

> Let us consecrate ourselves to the Immaculate Heart of Mary and work for the consecration of Russia to the Immaculate Heart of Mary. Certainly, Pope St. John Paul II consecrated the world, including Russia, to the Immaculate Heart of Mary on March 25, 1984. But, today, once again, we hear the call of Our Lady of Fatima to consecrate Russia to Her Immaculate Heart, in accord with her explicit instruction.[37]

Since then, it has been with the escalation of the Russo-Ukrainian war, when Russia invaded Ukraine in 2022, that the call for a repeat of the consecration was further heightened. Archbishop Mieczyslaw Mokrzycki of Lviv, Ukraine, told the Catholic News Agency on March 15, 2022,

> But Our Lady of Fatima in 1917 said that the consecration would be followed by a time of

---

[36] (Fr. David Francisquini, published in the Brazilian magazine Revista Catolicismo", no 836, Agosto/2020: "Was the Consecration of Russia Carried Out As Our Lady Requested"; cf 1Peter5.com

[37] https://voiceofthefamily.com/full-text-cardinal-burkes-historic-call-for-consecration-of-russia/

peace. That time of peace is now over, so we need to repeat the act of consecration of Russia and Ukraine… We believe that this act will be listened to by Our Lady and she will intercede before God for peace in Ukraine.[38]

Thus, on March 25, 2022, at the end of a penitential service in St. Peter's Basilica, Pope Francis carried out the act saying, "Mother of God and Our Mother, to Your Immaculate Heart we solemnly entrust and consecrate ourselves, the Church and all humanity, especially Russia and Ukraine." He did this in unity with the bishops around the world, in which a text of the prayer that Pope Francis utilized was sent out in advance. The act of consecration was also read simultaneously by Cardinal Konrad Krajewski, the papal almoner, at the sanctuary of Our Lady of Fatima in Portugal. In his homily that day, the Pope said that the consecration "is no magic formula but a spiritual act."[39]

So, did the required consecration of Russia happen? In my opinion, as Cardinal Raymond Burke noted above and Sr. Lucia indicated previously, the answer to that is yes, the consecration was fulfilled in 1984 by Pope John Paul II. Did the period of peace foretold at Fatima already occur? I would say it did (the peaceful breakup of the Soviet bloc was a tremendous event), but because the consecration was done so late it was not as efficacious (as

---

[38] Catholic News Agency, March 15, 2022, https://www.catholicnewsagency.com/news/250 684/ukrainian-archbishop-worldwide-novena-russia-consecration

[39] Catholic News Agency, March 25, 2022, Pope Francis consecrates Russia and Ukraine to the Immaculate Heart of Mary

far as lasting peace) as if it would have been done earlier. In other words, the peace after the 1984 consecration by Pope John Paul II was a definite event with the collapse of the Soviet Bloc but was not a complete peace nor long lasting. Thus, after this consecration by Pope John Paul II came the subsequent consecration of Russia and Ukraine to the Immaculate Heart of Mary by Pope Francis in 2022.

The key in understanding this whole process, in my opinion, is that it is a relationship between God and his people. In the year 2000, Pope John Paul II noted the significant challenges of our time but indicated that we would not be able to save ourselves or our world by utilizing "some magic formula" or by "inventing a new program."[40]

It is instead a relationship of God with his people. After Our Lady requested for the consecration of Russia to the Immaculate Heart of Mary in 1929, Our Lord was disappointed that it had not been done as of 1931. He indicated then that his ministers would "follow the example of the King of France in delaying the execution of My request" and that they would,

> …follow him into misfortune. Like the King of France, they will repent and do as I requested but it will be very late: Russia will already have spread her errors throughout the world causing wars and persecutions against the church. The Holy Father

---

[40] ("Formulam Veluti "Magicam", Pope John Paul II Apostolic Letter novo milenio ineunte, "at the close of the great jubilee of the year 2000", 6th January 2001, Boston: Pauline Books and Media, 2001, pg. 39, No. 29

will have much to suffer *but it will never be too late to have recourse to Jesus and Mary*" (italics for emphasis).

The end of that last line above, in my opinion, is exactly what these later consecrations turned out to be. They were recourses to Our Lord and to the Blessed Mother even though they were too late to prevent Russia from spreading her errors.

So we can see that it was "never too late to have recourse to Jesus and Mary" and that Our Lord did show mercy by fulfilling his promise to put an end to World War II. Russia, however, continued to spread her errors throughout the world. It is reasonable to assume that without this consecration of Pope Pius XII in 1942 that World War II may have gone on longer than it actually did.

This sequence of events occurred even more so with the actual confirmed consecration of Pope John Paul II in 1984. Our Lord again showed mercy with the subsequent fall of the Berlin wall and the breakup of the Soviet bloc. There was a relative political peace with the decline of overt communism. Nevertheless, Sister Lucia indicated in her letter to Pope John Paul II prior to the 1984 consecration that Russia had indeed already spread her errors all over the world. Even before the consecration was finally successfully accomplished, the evil had already spread worldwide.

As the evil has continued its spread, there was again most recently the call for Pope Francis to repeat the consecration with the goal of hopefully bringing the immense grace of God into the situation again. Since the completed consecration (of 1984) was accomplished so late, all that can apparently be asked for at this point forward is for a partial assistance which God indicated was still open to us. The partial assistance (ending of World War II rapidly and breakup of the Soviet bloc) were tremendous merciful graces, but in the end do not change the fact that we continue to live in this evil era which was foretold and which continues.

So again the question that titles this chapter arises, "Did the period of peace foretold at Fatima already happen?" I would again answer that with, "Yes, it did," but further add that there is a double meaning here. Why is there a double meaning? Because, in my opinion, the term "Russia" as utilized in the Fatima prophecy in 1917 now has a double meaning. Initially, prior to the spread of Communism, Russia as a nation and Russia as the seed of Communism were one and the same. If the consecration would have happened early on, the evil would have been nipped in the bud which would have been tremendous for worldwide lasting peace. Unfortunately, the consecration was instead done very late. With the spread of the "errors" of Russia now all over the world, the current meaning has been replaced; "Russia" in this context now also means the world. The fullness of peace was delayed because of the justice which still needs to play out from the lack of obedience in following Our Lord's request. The errors have to be played out to the level of completion only God knows. After that will come the substantial peace involving the whole world, the era of peace and triumph as also foretold by Our Lady of Good Success and Our Lady of La Salette.

After all, Our Lady noted as Our Lady Of Good Success that "I am Queen of Heaven under many invocations." Our Lady has come in many different forms, as noted in her multiple separate apparitions. In light of what she has revealed, especially as Our Lady of Good Success and Our Lady of La Salette, it makes sense to consider her statement from Fatima, "In the end, my Immaculate heart will triumph" with a resultant period of peace to also be interpreted as a future event occurring after this current era. So, in my opinion, the period of peace as foretold at Fatima has already occurred but also will be reoccurring, in a more substantial form, in the future.

Next, in further understanding what is going on in this chapter from a spiritual perspective, I would like to again touch on the similarities between the consecrations performed by the King of France and the Popes. This is an analogy which our Lord first referenced back in 1931 and which, in time, in my opinion, has only grown stronger. The similarities are very telling and I feel add a lot to the equation. For simplicity's sake they will be listed as follows:

1. France was linked to the Sacred Heart of Jesus while
1. Russia to the Immaculate Heart of Mary.
2. Both consecrations (by the Kings of France to the Sacred Heart and by the popes to the Immaculate Heart) needed to be done early. Our Lord was upset that the papal consecration of Russia was still not done after a fairly short period (by 1931, after the request for the consecration was given in 1929 for an apparition that occurred in 1917). Nevertheless, the years passed by and both were indeed done very late (100 years for France and greater than 50 years in the case of Fatima).

3. While Our Lord is merciful, he is also just. The tragic
4. latency and defiance of both the kings and popes in performing the consecrations has contributed to our current predicament.
5. France was a source of the Enlightenment utilizing the heresy of Deism which would have its adverse effects throughout the world. Russia was a source of Communism utilizing Atheism which would likewise have its adverse effects throughout the world. (It is interesting to note that Karl Marx, who grew up in Germany, was influenced by the Enlightenment.[41] We can see the domino effect of the errors of the Enlightenment building into the further errors of Communism.)
6. Both consecrations were done in accordance with the original request, but because of the very long latency, neither were as efficacious as they otherwise could have been. God grants us a window of time, and if that time is missed there can be consequences.
7. For King Louis XVI, it was a brush with death (placed under house arrest) and spreading of the rebellion (French Revolution) that resulted in his performing the thorough consecration to the Sacred Heart. For Pope John Paul II, it was a brush with death (being shot on the Feast of Fatima) and spreading of the rebellion (Sister Lucia informed him that the errors of Russia had already indeed

---

[41] Brittanica.com/biography/Karl-Marx

spread throughout the world) that resulted in his performing the thorough consecration to the Immaculate Heart.

8. The era we are currently living in is analogous to the four-year period of house arrest King Louis XVI lived after his consecration to the Sacred Heart but before his death. The evil is increasingly surrounding us, as it was him, and how long this era will last we do not know. (We do have a role in lessening the severity and shortening this evil timeframe with our prayers and actions, as has been previously noted and will be discussed later.)

9. The death of King Louis XVI is analogous to the death of our era. (Fortunately for us, Our Lady has promised a coming era of triumph as already discussed!)

So in wrapping up this chapter, we answered the initial question that yes, indeed, the period of peace foretold at Fatima occurred after the 1984 consecration. The dismantling of the Soviet bloc was a tremendous, merciful grace. Unfortunately, it was not a complete peace nor a long-lasting peace. The results were not as efficacious as hoped due to the fact that the consecration was very late. Our Lord is merciful and we should continue to come to him as it is "never too late to have recourse to Jesus and Mary." Nevertheless, our Lord is also just and, similar to the Kings of France, with the very late consecration there are consequences. The errors of Russia have indeed already spread throughout the whole world and we are thus continuing in this evil era which has been long foretold. There is a double meaning here which refers to another, future, more considerable peace that will occur with the triumph from our current era into the new era, as also described by Our Lady of Good Success and Our Lady of La Salette. "In the end, my Immaculate Heart will triumph" thus has two meanings, one which has happened already and the other, more substantial triumph which we await with anticipation!

Chapter 7

WHAT HAPPENS TO SATAN DURING THIS PERIOD OF PEACE?

We have been talking throughout this book about an upcoming era of peace. But what does this peace actually entail? Is it a type of heaven on earth, a utopia of sorts? Will there still be sin and suffering? What happens to the devil? After all, the St. Michael Prayer originated by Pope Leo XIII ends with, "By the divine power of God, cast into hell Satan and all evil spirits seeking the ruin of souls." So is that where the evil one goes during the era of peace, cast into hell? After all, how can you have a period of peace on earth when the devil is still active? Likewise, Our Lady of Good Success indicated that when the worst time of trial of this current era reaches its peak, when evil will seemed to have triumphed, that "This, then will mark the arrival of my hour, when I, in a marvelous way, will dethrone the proud and cursed Satan, trampling him under my feet and fettering him in the infernal abyss." The infernal abyss could certainly be another reference to hell. So, again, is that where Satan goes during this period of peace…to hell?

It appears that way when we initially look at how the Blessed Virgin Mary refers to the period of peace. Our Lady of La Salette indicated through the visionary Melanie that,

> Jesus Christ will be served, worshipped and glorified. Charity will flourish everywhere. The new kings will be the right arm of the Holy Church, which will be strong, humble, pious in its poor but fervent imitations of Jesus Christ. The Gospel will be preached everywhere and mankind will make great progress in its faith, for there will be unity among the workers of Jesus Christ and man will live in fear of God.

Many popes have given statements and teachings regarding a potential period of peace. An example includes Pope Pius XI who noted in his encyclical *Quas Primas* (1925),

> When once men recognize, both in private and public life, that Christ is King, society will at last receive the great blessings of real liberty, well ordered discipline, peace and harmony. ... If the kingdom of Christ, then, receives, as it should, all nations under its way, there seems no reason why we should despair of seeing that peace which the King of Peace came to bring on earth. ... Oh what happiness would be ours if all men, individuals, families and nations, would but let themselves be governed by Christ![42]

---

[42] Pope Pius XI encyclical on the Feast of Christ the King Quas

Another, more recent example is from the year 2000, at the World Day of Peace, when Pope John Paul II noted the following regarding a new era of peace: "God loves all men and women on earth and gives them the hope of a new era, an era of peace. His love, fully revealed in the incarnate Son, is the foundation of universal peace."[43]

The references above about this period of peace certainly sound appealing, but unfortunately with a closer glance not all is perfect. There is on the other hand biblical support for continued struggle with sin until the last day when Christ physically returns for his second coming. This can be seen in Matthew 13:24-30 when Jesus gives the parable of the wheat and the weeds, in which he teaches that the weeds will exist until "the harvest time." In Matthew 26:11, Jesus says, "You will always have the poor with you." In John 16:33, Jesus says, "In the world you have tribulation; but be of good cheer, I have overcome the world."

In addition, this teaching is distinctly described in Pope Paul VI's encyclical *Gaudium Et Spes* from 1965, "For a monumental struggle against the powers of darkness pervades the whole history of man. The battle was joined from the very origins of the world and will continue until the last day, as the Lord has attested" (paragraph 37).

So we are to have an upcoming period of peace but we are also going to continue to have a sinful world. With this conflicting information we are again lead back to the

---

Primas, 11th December 1925, 19

[43] Message of Pope John Paul II for the celebration of the World Day of Peace, January 1, 2000

same questions that were asked at the beginning of this chapter. How can we have a period of peace when we still have sin and suffering? And what happens to the devil? Is he really banished to hell? If he is banished to hell, where does the sin come from? If he is not banished to hell, how can we have peace?

In addressing these questions, I would like to present two biblical precedents that could shed some light on this topic. The first is in reference to the Book of Judges, with the cycle of unfaithfulness followed by faithfulness that is repeated by the ancient Israelites. The second precedent is from the Book of Job.

1. The Repeating Cycle of the Book of Judges:

In the Old Testament Book of Judges, the stories reveal ancient Israel's failure to live out the central demand of the covenant which is stated in the First Commandment, when the Lord tells us he is our God and we are to have no other gods before him.[44] The judges of the bible were military-type heroes who were spirit-led and could often be seriously flawed. Nevertheless, they rose up in times of crisis to lead the nation of Israel in battle against a threatening enemy.

The peoples' unfaithfulness to the First Commandment is played out in a type of cyclical drama that is often repeated and typically follows the same pattern:

> Act 1: Israel sins by neglecting the First Commandment and turning to other gods.

---

[44] Exodus 20:2-3

Act 2: God punishes Israel and allows an enemy to conquer it.

Act 3: The people repent and beg God for help and assistance.

Act 4: God sends someone who delivers them (a judge), who rescues Israel from the enemy.

While this template was applicable to ancient Israel, it is now, in my opinion, potentially analogous to the status of our current entire world. It could be conceived that we as a world are involved in this same four-act drama that was repeated by ancient Israel. For we, as a world, have turned away in many ways to other gods. We honor the gods of money, power, sensuality, materialism, or even our own selves, versus looking to the Almighty God. And like God punishing the ancient Israelites by not following the First Commandment, we likewise are under an era of trial and punishment. While the Israelites had a nearby human tribe as an enemy who conquered them, we instead have the spiritual enemy of the evil one who is being allowed and utilized by God in instituting our punishment. Thus, in this four-act play we currently are best categorized as being in Act II. God is punishing us because of our disobedience and allowing an enemy (the devil) to have increased power, with the movement towards Act III (where we, the people, repent and beg God for help and assistance). The question comes down to, how severe will the punishment be that we continue to suffer until there is an increased repentance and turning back towards God? Unlike the ancient Israelites, however, which only involved one nation and occurred repeatedly, this event has been foretold for centuries and involves the whole world.

In this case, the enemy is not another human tribe but Satan himself with his dominions. Thus, it makes sense that our deliverer in Act IV would not be a human judge as in the Old Testament, but instead a heavenly rescuer, in this case, the Immaculate Heart of Mary who with the Sacred Heart of Jesus will deliver those chosen to live into the era of peace.

2. The Book of Job:

In the Book of Job, Satan presented to God and challenged him specifically regarding the man Job, claiming that Job's righteousness was due to the blessings that God had bestowed upon him and his family. God, thus, granted Satan the power to put Job to the trial to see if he would blaspheme. After making it through a series of terrible trials and losing his wife, seven sons, three daughters, all of his possessions and essentially everything but his life, Job did not blaspheme God and was ultimately restored. In the restoration, the Lord blessed the later days of Job even more than his earlier ones. He doubled the number of sheep, camel and oxen compared to what Job had beforehand. He also gave Job a new wife and he blessed him again with seven sons and three daughters. Job then went on to live a long life with grandchildren and great-grandchildren.

The similarities with our current times can be seen with Satan approaching the throne of God, which reminds us of the vision of Pope Leo XIII sometime between 1884 and 1886 that resulted in the St. Michael

Prayer. Like Job, we as a church and as a world are now involved in an increased period of trial and suffering. While Job was noted to be righteous, the challenge was for him not to blaspheme God during all of his trials. We as a world have largely turned away from God and our challenge as a people is to turn back to him.

It becomes apparent in reading the Book of Job that at the end, during his restoration, Satan no longer has the power over Job which he had been given at the beginning. It would appear that Satan's power returned to its prior level. Job no longer goes through further severe sufferings and trials as before and in actuality his material possessions are doubled. This does not mean that the devil was not present during this era of Job's life, but that God nevertheless allowed the blessings and restoration to occur.

Likewise, those who are destined by God and make it through into the coming era of peace could see a time of increased joy and likely prosperity which God will allow in consoling his people. While the reality of sin will still be present, the recognition of God's merciful love in conquering sin will be much more apparent. While there will still be error, there will be greater insight into the truths of God in countering it. While suffering will still exist, it will much more frequently be joined to Christ and thus be redemptive in nature.

It is my opinion that during this period of peace, Satan's influence will be lessened as it appeared to be at the end of the Book of Job. While the St. Michael Prayer's ending calls out to God to "cast into hell Satan and all evil spirits who roam throughout the world seeking the ruin of souls," it is my opinion that this request is due to the devastating influence that Satan causes and the desire to rid us as much as possible of this influence. Likewise Our Lady of Good Success tells us, "… I, in a marvelous way, will dethrone the proud and cursed Satan, trampling him under my feet and fettering him in the infernal abyss." It would appear that Satan will not in actuality be thrown into the eternal abyss and no longer be present whatsoever on earth. It is instead that his level of increased power will be taken from him to a lesser level which will allow the faith to flourish. It is my opinion that some of the above statements are likely hyperbole or figurative language knowing the damage that Satan can do. It is not unlike Our Lord when he says in Mathew 5:29-30, "If your eye causes you to sin, pluck it out… If your hand causes you to sin, cut it off." Most theologians would indicate that this is not meant literally but is a hyperbole at how devastating sin can be.

After passing through the current trial we are experiencing, and with the subsequent lessening of the influence of Satan on earth, it will be much more possible for that which we request in the Our Father prayer to be realized. It is then that "Your will be done on earth as it is in heaven" will more likely be accomplished. People will of their own accord desire to do God's will on earth in this new era.

In essence, it is my opinion that this coming era of peace is similar to the end of the book of Job discussed above. The coming era of peace entails a lessening of the current power of Satan, at least to the prior level (i.e. before our current evil era) but not an elimination of the evil one's power altogether.

Chapter 8

Guidance and Hope for the Future

The Catholic Church in general is made up of three different sections: The Church Triumphant, the Church Suffering and the Church Militant. The Church Triumphant, of course, includes those who are in heaven, the Church Suffering includes the souls who are being purified in purgatory, and the Church Militant includes those of us Catholics who are still on earth fighting to overcome the imperfect and sinful dimensions of our existence. The times we are in, which have been long foretold, are making that fight even more challenging. But God has destined that each one of us is to be alive now, during this timeframe, when the evil one has been given even greater influence.

So what are we going to do? If we follow Christ, we are putting ourselves at odds with the world, a world which unfortunately has grown increasingly evil. As with Christ and the apostles, we may be challenged and suffer because of our faith and even potentially be martyred. You must weigh that as the cost you might pay.

We all have our fears, but we may nevertheless be called to answer the bell. In Judges 7:1 God told Gideon,

"Now announce to the army, 'Anyone who trembles with fear, turn back and leave Mount Gilead.'" So 22,000 men left. With that mass exodus only 10,000 men remained. Then Gideon pared the 10,000 down further to only 300 valiant men. As it ended up, Gideon was able to prevail over an enemy that vastly outnumbered his own men without having to fight.

This idea can also be seen in the Shakespeare play *Henry V* in the famous "Band of Brothers Speech." When confronting an enemy that greatly outnumbers him, it is suggested that Henry send for more troops back in England. Henry replies:

> The fewer the men, the greater share of honour … That he which hath no stomach to this fight, let him depart… We would not die in that man's company that fears his fellowship to die with us… From this day to the ending of the world … we in it shall be remembered … And gentleman in England now-a-bed shall think themselves accurs'd they were not here, and hold their manhoods cheap.[45]

But we say we don't have the courage. So it is with most of us. It's normal to have fears and concerns. Fortunately for us, God is always faithful and is there to give us courage. To quote 2 Thessalonians 3:3, "But the Lord is faithful, and he will strengthen you and protect you from the evil one."

---

[45] http://faculty.washington.edu/jwhelan/Documents/Speeches/St%20Cripins%20Day.pdf

While we are in this era surrounded by an increased evil influence, God has graciously sent Our Lady from Heaven to further guide and support us. In her maternal love she has visited us at these many different apparition sites over the centuries to inform us and to give us hope. We know that in the end, good indeed triumphs over evil and that a period of peace is on the horizon. Nevertheless, what has she told us we could be in for in the meantime?

Our Lady of Akita alerted us,

> As I told you, if men do not repent and better themselves, the Father will inflict a terrible punishment on all humanity. It will be a punishment greater than the deluge, such as one will never seen before. Fire will fall from the sky and will wipe out a great part of humanity, the good as well as the bad, sparing neither priests nor faithful. The survivors will find themselves so desolate that they will envy the dead. ...

Our Lady of Good Success noted,

> The small number of souls who, hidden, will preserve the treasure of the faith and the virtues will suffer a cruel, unspeakable and prolonged martyrdom. Many of them will succumb to death in the violence of the suffering, and those who sacrifice themselves for church and country will be counted as martyrs.

> In order to free men from bondage to these heresies, those whom the merciful love of my most Holy Son will destine for that restoration will need great strength of will, constancy, valor and much

confidence in God. To test this faith and confidence of the just, there will be occasions when everything will seem to be lost and paralyzed. This will be, then, the happy beginning of the complete restoration…

This, then, will mark the arrival of my hour, when I, in a marvelous way, will dethrone the proud and cursed Satan, trampling him under my feet and fettering him into the eternal abyss.

These above messages describe very concerning (if not downright scary) events! But with God, we need to remember that we don't have to fear. As it says in Psalm 23:4, "Even though I walk through the valley of the shadow of death, I will fear no evil, for you are with me; and your rod and your staff comfort me." The rod represents God's authority over all things and the staff represents, similar to a shepherd, God caring for his people.

We also can remember that God is ultimately in charge, no matter how bad things get. He can do anything if he so wills it. As Jesus said in Matthew 17:20-21, "Amen, I say to you, if you have faith the size of a mustard seed, you will say to this mountain, 'Move from here to there' and it will move. Nothing will be impossible for you."

He understands things way beyond our wildest imaginings. As it says in Isaiah 55:8-9,

'For my thoughts are not your thoughts, nor are your ways my ways,' declares the Lord. 'For as the heavens are higher than the earth, so are my ways higher than your ways and my thoughts than your thoughts.'

He tells us that we will never be abandoned. As David says in Psalm 16:8, "I know the Lord is always with me. I will not be shaken, for he is right beside me." God never forgets us; we are never alone. And Jesus further noted to his disciples, "And behold, I am always with you, to the end of the age."[46]

And he also wants what is best for us. As we are told in Psalm 37: 9-11, "Those who do evil will be cut off, but those who wait for the Lord will inherit the earth. Wait a little, and the wicked will be no more; look for them and they will not be there. But the meek will inherit the earth, will delight in great prosperity."

So we can be comforted that our all-powerful and all-knowing God wants what is best for us and will always be present for us no matter what happens. But, what do we do now? What has our Blessed Mother advised us to know and to do? As it turns out there are quite a few things that we can know and do. Here are some to make note of:

Jacinta from Fatima in one of her additional visions indicated the following:

> The sins of the world are very great. ... If men only knew what eternity is, they would do everything in their power to change their lives.... You must pray much for sinners and priests and religious.

Our Lady of Good Success further noted,

> If mortals understood how to appreciate the time given to them and would take advantage of each

---

[46] Matthew 28:20

moment of life, how different the world would be. And a considerable number of souls would not fall to their eternal perdition! This disdain is the fundamental cause of their downfall!

Our Lady of Fatima told Lucia in an additional vision in 1925,

> Look my daughter, at my heart, surrounded with thorns with which ungrateful men pierce me at every moment by their blasphemies and ingratitude. You at least try to console me and say that I promise to assist at the hour of death, with the graces necessary for salvation, all those who, on the first Saturday of five consecutive months, shall confess, receive holy communion, recite five decades of the Rosary, and keep me company for 15 minutes while meditating on the 15 mysteries of the Rosary, with the intention of making reparation to me.

We see this same message echoed decades later with Our Lady of Cuapa, "Renew the five first Saturdays. You received many graces when all of you did this."

Our Lady of Kibeho indicated that we must repent and convert. Our Lady of La Salette stressed the importance of honoring the sabbath both by attending Mass and ceasing to work on Sundays. At Betania Our Lady said, "…it is very important for you to attend Holy Mass frequently and to receive the Eucharist…so that My Divine Son's nourishment may help you…"

It is apparent that Our Lady wants us to remain in the state of grace under her mantel and to form good habits of regular Mass attendance, prayer, and frequent reception of the Sacrament of Reconciliation. We have a role in how this era plays out and the severity of the trials involved. I can't stress this enough. Each one of us has a role!

The Blessed Mother has continued to focus on the importance not only of frequent Mass attendance but also of praying the Rosary. Our Lady of Cuapa stressed the importance of praying the Rosary for all of the world. Our Lady of Akita reiterated, "Each day recite the prayers of the Rosary." At San Nicolas, Argentina, the title of Mary in that apparition is "Our Lady of the Rosary," a title also often given to Our Lady at Fatima. If there was one consistency through the many approved Marian apparitions throughout the centuries it would be the focus on praying the Rosary.

Yes, we are the Church Militant, and this is a call to arms. The Blessed Virgin Mary makes it clear that the Rosary is to be our weapon. Fellow soldier, I invite you to join me and pick up your beaded armament. There is no greater time than the present. Life is short, and regardless of what happens, we need to be spiritually prepared. Make the First Five Saturdays. Frequent the mass, even during the week if possible. Pray much for sinners and for priests and religious. Pray to God the Father that for the love and sacrifice of his Son he might take pity on us and bring an end to these ominous times. Stay in a state of grace, pray for perseverance and increased trust and guidance. Be confident in your knowledge that God is in charge and is always with you and will give you strength and courage. After all, God intended for you to be born for just such a time as this!

Appendix 1

Approved Apparition Inclusion vs. Exclusion

<u>Vatican Approved Marian Apparitions:</u>

- Guadalupe, Mexico (1531) - Our Lady of Guadalupe: Included (See Appendix 2.)
- Lezajsk, Poland (1578) - (Does not have a specific title.) Messages were given to a Polish woodcutter regarding building a church. It does not contain specific predictions for our era.
- Siluva, Lithuania (1608) - Our Lady of Siluva: Our Lady appeared to a number of children standing on a rock holding a baby in her arms and weeping bitterly. Multiple miracles were associated. The town which had lost its Catholic identity to the Calvinists over the course of 80 years was restored to the faith. No messages predicting our era were noted.
- Laus, France (1664) - Our Lady of Laus/Our Lady of Happy Meetings: Our Lady appeared to a poor shepherdess, asked for a church and house of priests to be built. Encouraged people to a greater conversion of faith and especially

focused on the sacrament of penance. Numerous physical healings have been associated with the site. No specific predictions for our era.

- Rue du Bac, Paris, France (1830) - Our Lady of the Miraculous Medal: Catherine Labouré received visions of the impending travails of France and detailing the designs for what would later be known as the Miraculous Medal. The messages did not include specific predictions for our era.

- Rome, Italy (1842) - Our Lady of The Miracle, or Our Lady of Zion: Marie-Alphonse Ratisbonne, who was an anti-Catholic, began wearing the Miraculous Medal as a simple test. While waiting in church for a baron that she had befriended, she encountered a vision of the Blessed Virgin Mary. The baron converted to Catholicism and joined the priesthood. There were no messages given to Marie Alphonse Ratisbonne.

- La Salette, France (1846) - Our Lady of La Salette: Included (See Appendix 4.)

- Lourdes, France (1858) - Our Lady of Lourdes: Our Lady appeared to St. Bernadette and called for penance and to pray for the conversion of sinners. Healings, conversions and miracles, including the incorrupt body of St. Bernadette are associated with this apparition. There is a healing ministry involving the waters of Lourdes. The messages were not specific as far as predictions for our era and thus it is not included.

- Filippsdorf, Czech Republic (1866) - Help of Christians: Magdalene Kade, an orphaned 31-year-old woman who was bedridden due to many illnesses, was healed after receiving a single vision of the Blessed Virgin Mary. The message of the apparition was related to the healing and there were no predictive messages regarding our era.

- Pontmain, France, (1871) - Our Lady of Hope: This single vision occurred during the Franco-Prussian war to a group of students at a convent school. The Prussians halted their advance when the commanders encountered "an invisible Madonna barring the way." There were no messages predictive of our times.

- Gietrzwald, Poland (1877) - Our Lady of Gietrzwald: Appearance to two girls requesting that the Rosary be said every day. The focus was to "pray the rosary zealously." The messages brought comfort to the Poles who were under oppression by Tsarist Russia. There were no messages related to our current times.

- Knock, Ireland (1879) - Our Lady of Knock: Mary, Joseph, John the Evangelist and the lamb were noted to appear in a village chapel enveloped by a bright light. None of them spoke. They occurred to 15 witnesses. There were no messages and thus no messages relating to our era.

- Fatima, Portugal (1917) - Our Lady of Fatima/Our Lady of the Rosary: Included (See Appendix 5.)
- Beauraing, Belgium (1932) - The Virgin with the Golden Heart: Mary appeared 33 times at the playground of a convent school to five children. She called for prayer and conversion of sinners. She asked that a chapel be built. During the later apparitions she revealed a heart of gold which was surrounded by rays. There were no messages related to our current times.
- Banneux, Belgium (1933) - The Virgin of the Poor: The Blessed Mother is said to have appeared to a child (Mariette Beco, age 11) eight times. She promised to intercede for the poor, the sick and the suffering. A spring was reserved to relieve the sick. She requested a small chapel. There were no messages specifically involving our times.
- Kibeho, Rwanda (1981) - Mother of the Word: Included (See Appendix 9.)

<u>Bishop Approved Marian Apparitions:</u>

- Quito, Ecuador (1594) - Our Lady of Good Success: Included (See Appendix 3.)
- Querrien, Bretania, France (1652) - Our Lady of Eternal Aid: Blessed Mother appeared to a young shepherdess who was born deaf and dumb. After the appearance she could speak and hear normally. She urged a chapel to be built.

There are no messages predictive of our era.

- Montagnaga, Italy (1729) - Madonna of Montagnaga: The Virgin was noted to appear to a shepherdess. She was described as having a Rosary in her hand and being dressed in white. No specific messages for our era were given.

- Robinsonville (now Champion), Wisconsin, USA (1859) - Our Lady of Good Help: The Blessed Mother appeared to a devout farm woman named Adele Brise and desired for Adele to teach others the Catechism and to evangelize. The chapel-enshrined property of Our Lady of Good Help was later the only place spared from a huge raging fire disaster. There were no messages predictive of our era.

- Castelpetroso, Italy (1888) - Our Lady of Sorrows: Our Lady was noted to appear to two shepherdesses and a healing spring appeared at the apparition site. There are noted similarities to the apparition site at Lourdes. There were no messages predictive of our era.

- Akita, Japan (1973) - Our Lady of Akita: Included (See Appendix 6.)

- Betania, Venezuela (1976) - Reconciler of People and Nations: Included (See Appendix 7.)

- Cuapa, Nicaragua (1980) - Our Lady of Cuapa: Included (See Appendix 8.)

- San Nicolas, Argentina (1983) - Our Lady of the Rosary: Included (See Appendix 10.)

Appendix 2

Our Lady of Guadalupe: Guadalupe, Mexico (1531)

(Note: This appendix is taken directly from EWTN's The Miracle Hunter website (http://www.miraclehunter.com) which gives a succinct timeline and description of the apparition and messages.)

Summary:

Mary proclaimed herself "the Mother of the true God who gives life" and left her image permanently upon the tilma of St. Juan Diego, a man newly converted to Christianity. Her likeness was given as a sign to Bishop Zumarraga, who abided by her wishes and constructed a church on Mt. Tepeyacac, the site of the apparitions. Millions of natives were converted to Christianity during the period following her visit. Our Lady of Guadalupe has been designated as the Patron Saint of the Americas.

Timeline

12/9/1531	The Virgin appeared to Juan Diego on top of mount Tepeyacac speaking to him in Nahuatl, his native tongue. She called him "Xocoyte," her little son. She requests that he petition the bishop of Mexico that a "teocalli" a sacred little house, be built on the spot. Juan Diego, calling her "Xocoyata," his littlest daughter, agrees to comply with her mandate and meets with the bishop who listens to the message but does not believe his words. On his return he encounters the Virgin again who insists that he return to the bishop with the same message the next day.
12/10/1531	Juan does not return to the bishop the next day because his uncle Juan Bernardino takes ill and requests Juan Diego to find a priest for his final confession.
12/11/1531	Juan goes from his home to Tlatelolco to summon a priest and despite trying to avoid her, encounters along the way the Virgin who promises that his uncle will be cured. She urges him to climb to the top of the hilltop and gather the roses growing there in December as the sign for the bishop to believe. When the Bishop finally received him, Juan unfurled his tilma and revealed the image of the Virgin miraculously painted there.
12/12/1531	Juan Diego shows the bishop the location of the apparition on which the church was to be built. He then returned

	to his uncle who was cured of his illness and had experienced a visitation from the Virgin himself.

Messages:

The Blessed Virgin appeared four times to Juan Diego. In her messages she asked for his obedience in petitioning Bishop Zumarraga erect a church on the hill of Tepeyacac.

(Excerpted from an English translation of Luis Lasso de la Vega's 1649 copy of the *Nican Mopohua* written in Nahuatl by the Indian scholar Antonio Valeriano in the mid-16th century.)

First Apparition (Saturday):

The Blessed Virgin: "Juanito, the most humble of my sons, where are you going?"

Juan Diego: "My Lady and Child, I have to reach your church in Mexico, Tlatelolco, to pursue things divine, taught and given to us by our priests, delegates of Our Lord."

The Virgin: "Know and understand well, you the most humble of my son, that I am the ever virgin Holy Mary, Mother of the True God for whom we live, of the Creator of all things, Lord of heaven and the earth. I wish that a temple be erected here quickly, so I may therein exhibit and give all my love, compassion, help, and protection, because I am your merciful mother, to you, and to all the inhabitants on this land and all the rest who love me, invoke and confide in me; listen there to their lamentations, and remedy all their miseries, afflictions and sorrows. And to accomplish what my clemency pretends, go to the palace of the bishop of Mexico, and you will say to him that I manifest my great desire, that here on this plain a temple be built to me; you will accurately relate all you have seen and admired, and what you have heard. Be assured that I will be most grateful and will reward you, because I will make you happy and worthy of recompense for the effort and fatigue in what you will obtain of what I have entrusted. Behold, you have heard my mandate, my humble son; go and put forth all your effort."

Juan Diego: "My Lady, I am going to comply with your mandate; now I must part from you, I, your humble servant."

Second Apparition (Saturday):

Juan Diego: "Lady, the least of my daughters, my Child, I went where you sent me to comply with your command. With difficulty I entered the prelate's study. I saw him and exposed your message, just as you instructed me. He received me benevolently and listened attentively, but when he replied, it appeared that he did not believe me. He said: "You will return; I will hear you at my pleasure. I will review from the beginning the wish and desire which you have brought." I perfectly understood by the manner he replied that he believes it to be an invention of mine that you wish that a temple be built here to you, and that it is not your order; for which I exceedingly beg, Lady and my Child, that you entrust the delivery of your message to someone of importance, well known, respected, and esteemed, so that they may believe in him;

because I am a nobody, I am a small rope, a tiny ladder, the tail end, a leaf, and you, my Child, the least of my children, my Lady, you send me to a place where I never visit nor repose. Please excuse the great unpleasantness and let not fretfulness befall, my Lady and my All."

The Blessed Virgin: "Hark, my son the least, you must understand that I have many servants and messengers, to whom I must entrust the delivery of my message, and carry my wish, but it is of precise detail that you yourself solicit and assist and that through your mediation my wish be complied. I earnestly implore, my son the least, and with sternness I command that you again go tomorrow and see the bishop. You go in my name, and make known my wish in its entirety that he has to start the erection of a temple which I ask of him. And again tell him that I, in person, the ever-virgin Holy Mary, Mother of God, sent you."

Juan Diego: "Lady, my Child, let me not cause you affliction. Gladly and willingly I will go to comply your mandate. Under no condition will I fail to do it, for not even the way is distressing. I will go to do your wish, but perhaps I will not be heard with liking, or if I am heard I might not be believed. Tomorrow afternoon, at sunset, I will come to bring you the result of your message with the prelate's reply. I now take leave, my Child, the least, my Child and Lady. Rest in the meantime."

Third Apparition (Sunday):

The Blessed Virgin: "Well and good, my little dear, you will return here tomorrow, so you may take to the bishop the sign he has requested. With this he will believe you, and in this regard he will not doubt you nor will he be suspicious of you; and know, my little dear, that I will reward your solicitude and effort and fatigue spent on my behalf. Lo! go now. I will await you here tomorrow."

Fourth Apparition (Tuesday):

The Blessed Virgin Mary: "What's there, my son the least? Where are you going?"

Juan Diego: "My Child, the most tender of my daughters, Lady, God grant you are content. How are you this morning? Is your health good, Lady and my Child? I am going to cause you grief. Know, my Child, that a servant of yours is very sick, my uncle. He has contracted the plague, and is near death. I am hurrying to your house in Mexico to call one of your priests, beloved by our Lord, to hear his confession and absolve him, because, since we were born, we came to guard the work of our death. But if I go, I shall return here soon, so I may go to deliver your message. Lady and my Child, forgive me, be patient with me for the time being. I will not deceive you, the least of my daughters. Tomorrow I will come in all haste."

The Blessed Virgin Mary: "Hear me and understand well, my son the least, that nothing should frighten or grieve you. Let not your heart be disturbed. Do not fear that sickness, nor any other sickness or anguish. Am I not here, who is your mother? Are you not under my protection? Am I not your health? Are you not happily within my fold? What else do you wish? Do not grieve nor be disturbed by anything. Do not be afflicted by the illness of your uncle, who will not die now of it. be assured that he is now cured."

"Climb, my son the least, to the top of the hill; there where you saw me and I gave you orders, you will find different flowers. Cut them, gather them, assemble them, then come and bring them before my presence."

"My son the least, this diversity of roses is the proof and the sign which you will take to the bishop. You will tell him in my name that he will see in them my wish and that he will have to comply to it. You are my ambassador, most worthy of all confidence. Rigorously I command you that only before the presence of the bishop will you unfold your mantle and disclose what you are carrying. You will relate all and well; you will tell that I ordered you to climb to the hilltop, to go and cut flowers; and all that you saw and admired, so you can induce the prelate to give his support, with the aim that a temple be built and erected as I have asked."

<u>Miracles and Signs:</u>

The tilma was made from cactus fibers and as such should have turned into dust after approximately twenty years. Instead it has survived and been on display to the faithful for nearly 500 years despite being exposed to the smoke of candles throughout the centuries. Infrared spectroscopy has confirmed the integrity of the image.

The image on the tilma is composed of pigments that have not been identified by chemical analysis as being the product of animal, vegetable, or mineral dye. No under sketch has been identified below the painting.

Examination of the eyes of the image by photographers and ophthalmologists has suggested that the reflections of Juan Diego, the bishop, and the interpreter can be distinguished.

Additionally, the apparitions and the resulting tilma contributed in no small way to the Christianization of Mexico with several million Aztecs converting to Christianity in the ensuing years.

Visionary:

St. Juan Diego was born in 1474 with the name "Cuauhtlatoatzin" ("the talking eagle") in Cuautitlán, today part of Mexico City, Mexico. He was a gifted member of the Chichimeca people, one of the more culturally advanced groups living in the Anáhuac Valley.

When he was 50 years old he was baptized by a Franciscan priest, Fr Peter da Gand, one of the first Franciscan missionaries. On 9 December 1531, the Blessed Mother appeared to him on Tepeyac Hill, the outskirts of what is now Mexico City.

With the Bishop's permission, Juan Diego lived the rest of his life as a hermit in a small hut near the chapel where the miraculous image was placed for veneration. Here he cared for the church and the first pilgrims who came to pray to the mother of Jesus.

Church Approval:

In 1555 In the Provincial Counsel, the second archbishop of Mexico, Alonso de Montúfar, formulated canons that indirectly approved the apparitions. A formal inquiry and investigation was conducted by the Church from February 18 to March 22, 1666, and again by Archbishop Lanziego y Eguilaz in 1723.

Juan Diego was beatified on May 6, 1990, and canonized by Pope John Paul II on July 31, 2002. His feast day is December 9th.

Pope John Paul II, during his third visit to the sanctuary on March 25, 1999, declares the date of December the 12th as a Liturgical Holy Day for the whole continent.

The Feast Day of Our Lady of Guadalupe is December 12th.

Shrines:

- Basilica de Santa Maria de Guadalupe - Mexico City, Mexico
- Shrine of Our Lady of Guadalupe - Diocese of La Crosse, WI, USA
- Our Lady of Guadalupe Chapel - National Shrine of the Immaculate Conception in Washington, D.C.

Appendix 3

Our Lady of Good Success: Quito, Ecuador (1594)

(Note: This appendix is taken directly from EWTN's The Miracle Hunter website (http://www.miraclehunter.com) which gives a succinct timeline and description of the apparition and messages.)

Summary:

Our Lady of Good Success appeared to Spanish-born Mother Mariana de Jesus Torres at her Conceptionist Royal Convent in Quito, Ecuador. She requested that a statue be made in her likeness and warned of diminishing faith and vocations in the 20th century.

Timeline

1563	Mariana de Jesus Torres is born.
1577	A small group of religious sisters and a 13-year-old girl with a vocation (Mariana) completes an arduous journey by ship from Spain to Ecuador to found the first convent in Quito,

	Ecuador.
1582	Mariana dies for the first time. Once in Heaven she chose to return to earth to suffer as an expiratory victim for the sins of the 20th century.
1588	Her second death was on Good Friday after an apparition where she was shown the horrible abuses and heresies that would exist in the Church in our times. She was resurrected two days later on Easter Sunday morning.
2/2/1594	Our Lady of Good Success first appears to Mariana
1/16/1599	Our Lady of Good Success requests a statue to be made to her likeness.
1605-1610	Due an upheaval in the convent caused by an unfaithful and rebellious sister who incited some of sisters against Mother Mariana, Mariana chose to take on 5 years of the suffering and punishments of hell that this sister would have had to endure. Later the rebellious sister repented for her ways.
1/16/1611	The sculptor chosen by Our Lady, Francisco del Castillo, leaves town to purchase the final paints for the statue. At 3:00 AM, Our Lady of Good Success appears with the Archangels Michael, Gabriel and Raphael along with St. Francis to complete the statue. The archangels bowed down to Mary and sang a prayer: "Hail to Thee, Mary Most Holy Daughter of God the Father" (St. Michael)

	"Hail to Thee, Mary Most Holy Mother of God the Son" (St. Gabriel)
	"Hail to Thee, Mary Most Holy Most Pure Spouse of the Holy Ghost" (St. Raphael)
	"Hail to Thee, Mary Most Holy Temple and Sacrarium of the Most Holy Trinity" (All three Archangels)
	With this, the statue of Our Lady was completed. The statue became animated as Mary walked into the statue itself. Our Lady of Good Success began to sing the "Magnificat." A choir of heavenly spirits began to sing "Salve Sancta Parens" which awakened the rest of the convent. The sisters rushed to the choir loft and found the statue transformed and surrounded by a heavenly light.
2/2/1611	The statue is officially blessed by the bishop. Our Lady of Good Success was placed above the seat of the Abbess chair at her own specific request as a sign to all that she was the one who governed and watched over the convent. Her official title being that of "Mary of Good Success of the Purification."
1611	Our Lord appeared to Mother Mariana and asked her to be victim soul: "For all times I have need of valiant souls to save my Church and the prevaricating world."

2/2/1634	Feast of the Purification, the 40th anniversary of the first appearance of Our Lady of Good Success to Mother Mariana.
12/8/1634	On the feast of the Immaculate Conception, three archangels and their Queen appeared to Mother Mariana. St. Gabriel was carrying a ciborium filled with Hosts. Our Lady predicts several events in the future Papacy of Blessed Pope Pius IX.
1/16/1635	After receiving Holy Communion and the Last Rites, she foretold the exact hour of her death (3 PM) and died for the final time.
1821	The "truly Catholic" president of Ecuador, Gabriel Garcia Moreno foretold by Our Lady is born.
1873	Gabriel Garcia Moreno consecrated the republic to the Sacred Heart of Jesus.
1875	Gabriel Garcia Moreno dies. Pope Pius IX paid him tribute as a man who died "the death of a martyr…a victim to his Faith and Christian charity." In the Cathedral of Quito there is a display of Gabriel Moreno's incorrupt heart and the famous painting of Our Lady of Quito, which wept at the moment of his martyrdom.
1906	During then remodeling of the Convent, Mother Mariana's three-century old tomb was opened. Her body and habit were found to be whole and incorrupt.

1941	A prayer to Our Lady of Good Success received the imprimatur of a bishop, Carlos Maria Javier de la Torre, archbishop of Quito, who provided it in 1941 as a partial approval.
1986	A cause for beautification of Mother Mariana was launched.
1991	The archbishop of Quito, Antonio José González Zumárraga, petitioned Rome for and received a canonical coronation of Our Lady of Good Success as "Queen of Quito."
1991	The Conceptionist Convent in Quito was made an Archdiocesan Marian Sanctuary.

Description of the Virgin:

In an apparition to Mother Mariana de Jesus Torres, the Blessed Virgin appeared and asked that a statue be made of her under the title of Good Success. She should be made just as she appeared to her there, with the Child Jesus in her right arm, and the Abbess' crozier and the keys of the Convent in her right hand. She should be placed above the Abbess chair in the upper choir because she desired to be Abbess of that Convent until the end of time. And so the Virgin of Good Success of Quito appears with the crozier in her right hand, instead of the scepter that she carries in Madrid.

Messages:

The messages of Our Lady of Good Success spoke of the worldwide crisis in the Church and society that would begin in the 19th century and extend throughout the 20th century. During that time, she warned, there would be an almost total corruption of customs and Satan would rule almost completely by means of the Masonic sects. In the Catholic Church, the Sacraments would be profaned and abused, and the light of Faith would be almost completely extinguished in souls. Truly religious souls would be reduced to a small number and many vocations would perish. Great impurity would reign and people would be without any care for spiritual matters.

The Messages of Quito:

Excerpts taken from the 18th Century manuscript entitled The Admirable Life of Mother Mariana of Jesus Torres, written a century after her death by Prior Manuel de Souza Pereira, Franciscan Provincial in Quito, Ecuador and director of the Convent Mother Mariana founded.

February 2, 1594:

"I am Mary of Good Success, who you have invoked with such tender affection. Your prayer has pleased me very much. Your faith has brought me here. Your love has invited me to visit you…"

January 16, 1599:

"…now I ask and command you to have a statue to be made for the consolation and preservation of my convent and for those faithful souls of that epoch during which there will be a great devotion to me, for I am the Queen of Heaven under many invocations…With the making of this statue I will favor not only my convent, but also the people of Quito – and all the people throughout the centuries."

"First so that men in the future might realize how powerful I am in placating Divine Justice and obtaining mercy and pardon for every sinner who comes to me with a contrite heart. For I am the Mother of Mercy and in me there is only goodness and love."

"And second…when tribulations of spirit and sufferings of the body oppress them and they seem to be drowning in this bottomless sea let them gaze at my holy image and I will always be there ready to listen to their cries and soothe their pain. Tell them that they should always run to their Mother with confidence and love…"

January 16, 1611:

St. Michael said: "Hail to Thee, Mary Most Holy Daughter of God the Father"

St. Gabriel said: "Hail to Thee, Mary Most Holy Mother of God the Son"

St. Raphael said: "Hail to Thee, Mary Most Holy, Most Pure Spouse of the Holy Ghost"

All together they chanted: "Hail to Thee, Mary Most Holy Temple and Sacrarium of the Most Holy Trinity"

Our Lady:

"Against them the impious will rage a cruel war, overwhelming them with vituperations, calumnies and vexations in order to stop them from fulfilling their ministry. But they, like firm columns, will remain unswerving and will confront everything with a spirit of humility and sacrifice with which they will be vested, by virtue of the infinite merits of my most Holy Son, Who will love them in the innermost fibers of His Most Holy and Tender Heart."

"The small number of souls, who hidden, will preserve the treasures of the Faith and practice virtue will suffer a cruel, unspeakable and prolonged martyrdom. Many will succumb to death from the violence of their sufferings and those who sacrifice themselves for the Church and their country will be counted as martyrs. In order to free men from the bondage to these heresies, those whom the merciful love of my most Holy Son has designated to effect the restoration, will need great strength of will, constancy, valor and confidence of the just. There will be occasions when all will seem lost and paralyzed. This then will be the happy beginning of the complete restoration."

"Under the appearance of virtue and bad-spirited zeal, would turn upon Religion, who nourished them at her breast." "During this time insomuch as this poor country will lack the Christian spirit, the Sacrament of Extreme Unction will be little esteemed. Many people will die without receiving it either because of the negligence of their families or their false sentimentality that tries to protect the sick from seeing the gravity of their situations, or because they will rebel against the spirit of the Catholic Church, impelled by the malice of the devil. Thus many souls will be deprived of innumerable graces, consolations and the strength they need to make that great leap from time to eternity…"

"As for the Sacrament of Matrimony, which symbolizes the union of Christ with His Church, it will be attacked and profaned in the fullest sense of the word.

Masonry, which will then be in power, will enact iniquitous laws with the objective of doing away with this Sacrament, making it easy for everyone to live in sin, encouraging the procreation of illegitimate children born without the blessing of the Church. The Christian spirit will rapidly decay, extinguishing the precious light of Faith until it reaches the point that there will be an almost total and general corruption of customs. The effects of secular education will increase, which will be one reason for the lack of priestly and religious vocations…"

"The Sacred Sacrament of Holy Orders will be ridiculed, oppressed and despised. … The demon will try to persecute the Ministers of the Lord in every possible way and he will labor with cruel and subtle astuteness to deviate them from the spirit of their vocation, corrupting many of them. These corrupted priests, who will scandalize the Christian people, will incite the hatred of the bad Christians and the enemies of the Roman, Catholic and Apostolic Church to fall upon all priests. This apparent triumph of Satan will bring enormous sufferings to the good Pastors of the Church…"

"Moreover, in these unhappy times, there will be unbridled luxury which, acting thus to snare the rest into sin, will conquer innumerable frivolous souls who will be lost. Innocence will almost no longer be found in children, nor modesty in women, and in this supreme moment of need of the Church, those who should speak will fall silent."

"But know, beloved daughter, that when your name is made known in the 20th century, there will be many who will not believe, claiming that this devotion is not pleasing to God… A simple humble faith in the truth of My apparitions to you, My predilect child, will be reserved for humble and fervent souls docile to the inspirations of grace, for Our Heavenly Father communicates His secrets to the simple of heart, and not to those whose hearts are inflated with pride, pretending to know what they do not, or self-satisfied with empty knowledge."

"The secular Clergy will leave much to be desired because priests will become careless in their sacred duties. Lacking the divine compass, they will stray from the road traced by God for the priestly ministry, and they will become attached to wealth and riches, which they will unduly strive to obtain. How the Church will suffer during this dark night! Lacking a Prelate and Father to guide them with paternal love, gentleness, strength, wisdom and prudence, many priests will lose their spirit, placing their souls in great danger. This will mark the arrival of My Hour."

"Therefore, clamor insistently without tiring and weep with bitter tears in the privacy of your heart, imploring our Celestial Father that for love of the Eucharistic Heart of my Most Holy Son and His precious Blood shed with such generosity and the profound bitterness and sufferings of His cruel Passion and Death, He might take pity on His ministers and bring to an end those Ominous times, sending to this Church the Prelate who will restore the spirit of its priests."

December 8, 1634:

"This signifies the Most August Sacrament of the Eucharist, which will be distributed by my Catholic priests to faithful Christians belonging to the Holy

Roman, Catholic and Apostolic Church whose visible head is the Pope, the King of Christianity. His pontifical infallibility will be declared a dogma of the Faith by the same Pope chosen to proclaim the dogma of the Mystery of My Immaculate Conception. He will be persecuted and imprisoned in the Vatican by the unjust usurpation of the Pontifical States through the iniquity, envy and avarice of an earthly monarch."

"In the 19th Century there will be a truly Catholic president, a man of character whom God Our Lord will give the palm of martyrdom on the square adjoining this Convent. He will consecrate the Republic to the Sacred Heart of My Most Holy Son, and this consecration will sustain the Catholic Religion in the years that follow, which will be ill-fated ones for the Church. These years, during which the evil sect of Masonry will take control of the civil government will see a cruel persecution of all religious communities, and they will also strike out violently against this one of mine."

Prophecies:

On December 8, 1634, the feast of the Immaculate Conception, three archangels and their Queen appeared to Mother Mariana. St. Gabriel was carrying a Ciborium filled with Hosts which Our lady explained: "This signifies the Most August Sacrament of the Eucharist, which will be distributed by my Catholic priests to faithful Christians belonging to the Holy Roman, Catholic and Apostolic Church, whose visible head is the Pope, the King of Christianity. His pontifical infallibility will be declared a dogma of the Faith by the same Pope chosen to proclaim the dogma of the Mystery of My Immaculate Conception. He will be persecuted and imprisoned in the Vatican by the unjust usurpation of the Pontifical States through the iniquity, envy and avarice of an earthly monarch." This holy Pope was Blessed Pius IX, who fulfilled every prediction made by Our Lady.

Another most interesting prophecy of Our Lady: "In the 19th Century there will be a truly Catholic president, a man of character whom God Our Lord will give the palm of martyrdom on the square adjoining this Convent. He will consecrate the Republic to the Sacred Heart of My Most Holy Son, and this consecration will sustain the Catholic Religion in the years that will follow, which will be ill-fated ones for the Church. These years, during which the evil sect of Masonry will take control of the civil government will see a cruel persecution all religious communities, and they will also strike out violently against this one of mine."

The "truly Catholic" president of Ecuador, Gabriel Garcia Moreno (1821-1875), consecrated the republic to the Sacred Heart of Jesus in 1873. Pope Pius IX paid him tribute as a man who had died "the death of a martyr…a victim to his Faith and Christian charity." In the Cathedral of Quito there is a display of Gabriel Moreno's incorrupt heart and the famous painting of Our Lady of Quito, which wept at the moment of his martyrdom.

Miracles and Signs:

One of the most extraordinary facts of her life was a mystical-physical phenomenon: her several deaths and resurrections. Documented records from the Convent and Diocesan archives show that this truly holy religious died three times. Her first death was in 1582. Standing before the Judgment Seat, she was judged blameless and given a choice: to remain in celestial glory in Heaven or to return to earth to suffer as an expiratory victim for the sins of the 20th century. She chose the latter. Her second death was on Good Friday of 1588 after an apparition where she was shown the horrible abuses and heresies that would exist in the Church in our times. She was resurrected two days later on Easter Sunday morning. She finally died on January 16, 1635. At her wake, a blind girl was cured.

In 1906, during remodeling of the Convent, her three-century old tomb was opened. They discovered the body of Mother Mariana de Jesus whole and incorrupt, complete with her habit and the articles of penance that had been placed in the tomb with her. As exquisite aroma of lilies emanated from her whole body.

Church approval:

Bishop Salvador de Ribera of Quito attested in official documents to the miraculous completion of the Statue by St. Francis of Assisi and the three Archangels – St. Michael, St. Gabriel and St. Raphael – and presided over the anointing of the solemn consecration of the Statue in the Church of the Royal Convent of the Immaculate Conception on February 2, 1611. The devotion and apparitions were also authorized and promoted by the next Bishop of Quito, Pedro de Oviedo, who governed the Diocese from 1630 to 1646.

A prayer to the Our Lady of Good Success has the imprimatur of a bishop, Carlos Maria, archbishop of Quito, who provided it in 1941 as a partial approval.

The Feast of Our Lady of Good Success is celebrated on February 2nd, the Feast of the Purification of Mary.

Appendix 4

Our Lady of La Salette: La Salette, France (1846)

(Note: This appendix is taken directly from EWTN's The Miracle Hunter website (http://www.miraclehunter.com) which gives a succinct timeline and description of the apparition and messages.)

Summary:

Six Thousand feet up in the French Alps, the Blessed Virgin Mary is believed to have come to 11-year-old Maximin Giraud and 14-year-old Melanie Calvat-Mathieu while they tended sheep. Her appearance in sorrow and tears called for conversion and penance for sins.

Timeline:

Nov 7, 1831	Melanie Calvat-Mathieu is born in Corps, France.
Aug 26, 1835	Maximin Giraud is born in Corps, France.
Sept 19, 1846	Melanie and Maximin are out tending sheep and encounter a glowing globe of light. A beautiful weeping woman wearing a high headdress of roses, a

	silver robe, a gold apron, white shoes, and a golden crucifix hanging from a chain around her neck, appears sitting on a rock and she relates how the offenses of men such as not reverencing the name of God and work on Sundays will result in calamities, including a potato famine in 1846-7 and disease. The woman entrusts each child with a secret and encourages them to pray and then ascends the hill and disappears.
Sept 1846	The bishop of the diocese, Mgr Philibert de Bruillard of Grenoble, begins the official inquiry into the phenomenon.
Oct 1846	The prophecies of La Salette are widely circulated.
August 1848	Father Rousselot, Vicar General of Grenoble, and appointed reporter on the apparitions, answers twelve objections to the truth of the events in his report entitled "The Truth about the event of La Salette" was addressed to Pope Pius IX
July 3, 1851	Cardinal Boland, archbishop of Lyon, remained skeptical and Maximin and Melanie were made to record the secret given to each of them in the presence of Church officials and deliver their statement to the Bishop.
July 6, 1851	Melanie rewrites the Secret to fix a chronological error she identified in her original and re-submits her statement to the Bishop.

July 18, 1851	The documentary letters are transmitted to Pope Pius IX by two accredited messengers, MM. Rousselot and Gérin. The secret is placed in the archives of the Vatican.
Sept 19, 1851	Mgr de Bruillard publishes a pastoral letter for the fifth anniversary of the Apparition in which he affirmed that the apparition "has within itself all the characteristics of the truth, and that the faithful are justified in believing it beyond doubt and for certain"
1851	Melanie became a nun taking the name Sister Mary of the Cross with the Sisters of Providence and then transferred to the Sisters of Charity.
May 1, 1852	Mgr de Bruillard announces in a pastoral letter the erection of a shrine on the mountain of the Apparition and the institution of the Missionaries of Our Lady of La Salette, commissioned to serve the shrine.
May 25, 1852	The first stone of The Shrine of La Salette was blessed by Mgr de Bruillard. The Shrine was built near the location of the apparition at the center of a mountain ring formed by the Gargas and the Chamoux.
May 1853	Mgr Ginoulhiac, is appointed bishop of Grenoble after the resignation of Mgr de Bruillard.
Nov 4, 1854	The Bishop issues a pastoral letter which condemned a memorandum published in Grenoble addressed to the Pope against the judgement of

	1851. Ginoulhiac additionally renews his predecessor's doctrinal judgement in a more explicit and this time definitive way.
1855	Melanie was allowed to transfer to an English Carmelite convent.
1860	The local bishop forbade her from speaking publicly so she returned to France to join a convent at Marseille.
1867	Her identity was discovered and she left for Naples. In Naples, she wrote down the secret for the Order of the Apostles of the Last Days (men) and Order of the Mother of God (women).
Dec 26, 1870	Melanie writes a letter to Fr Bliard.
Aug 18, 1872	700 pilgrims from Paris, later joined by other groups from Dijon, Ars and Lyons, participate in France's First National Pilgrimage and travel to La Salette.
March 1, 1875	Death of Maximin. He had entered the seminary but never reached ordination.
Nov 15, 1879	Last manuscript of the secret of La Salette written by Melanie in 1873 and published in 1879 as a booklet with the imprimatur of Bishop Salvatore Luigi Zola entitled *Apparition of the Blessed Virgin on the Mountain of La Salette*. This version of the secret is much longer and contains more detail. It also predicted the future apostacy of Rome.
1879	The completed basilica was consecrated.

Dec 15, 1904	Death of Melanie in Naples
1923	Melanie's secret of 1879 was placed on the *Index of Forbidden Books*
October 1999	Melanie's 1851 secret was rediscovered by Fr Michel Corteville in the Vatican Archives.

Messages:

The central theme of the Virgin's messages was turn away from sin and do penance or undergo terrible suffering.

"Come to me, my children. Do not be afraid. I am here to tell you something of the greatest importance. If my people will not obey, I shall be compelled to loose my Son's arm. It is so heavy, so pressing that I can no longer restrain it."

"How long I have suffered for you! If my Son is not to cast you off, I am obliged to entreat Him without ceasing. But you take no least notice of that. No matter how well you pray in future, no matter how well you act, you will never be able to make up to me what I have endured for your sake."

" 'I have appointed for you six days for working. The seventh I have reserved for myself. And no one will give it to me.' This is what causes the weight of my Son's arm to be so crushing."

"The cart drivers cannot swear without bringing in my Son's name. These are two things that make my Son's arm so burdensome. If the harvest is spoiled it is your fault. I warned you last year (1845) by means of the potatoes. You paid no heed. Quite the reverse, when you discovered that the potatoes had rotted, you swore, you abused my Son's name. They will continue to rot and by Christmas this year there will be none left."

"If you have grain, it will do you no good to sow it, for what you sow the beasts will devour, and any part of it that springs up will crumble into dust when you thresh it. A great famine is coming. But before that happens, the children under seven years of age will be seized with trembling and die in their parents' arms. The grownups will pay for their sins by hunger. The grapes will rot and the walnuts will turn bad…."

"If people are converted, the rocks will become piles of wheat, and it will be found that the potatoes have sown themselves….

"Only a few rather old women go to Mass in the summer. All the rest work every Sunday throughout the summer. And in winter, when they don't know what to do with themselves, they go to Mass only to poke fun at religion. During Lent they flock to the butcher shops, like dogs…..My children, you will make this known to all people."

The Priests, the ministers of my Son, the priests by their wicked lives, by their irreverence and their impiety in the celebration of the holy mysteries, by their love of money, their love of honors and pleasures, the priests have become cesspools of impurity. Yes, the priests are asking for vengeance, and vengeance is hanging over their heads. Woe to the priests and those dedicated to God who by their infidelity and their wicked lives are crucifying My Son again! The sins of those consecrated to God cry out towards heaven and call for vengeance, and now vengeance is at their door, for there is no one left to beg mercy and forgiveness for the people. There are no generous souls, there is no one left worthy of offering a spotless sacrifice to the Eternal on behalf of the world."

"God will strike in an unprecedented way."

"Woe to the inhabitants of the earth! God will exhaust his wrath upon them, and no one will be able to escape so many afflictions altogether."

"The chiefs, the leaders of the people of God have neglected prayer and penance, and the devil has bedimmed their intelligence. They have become wandering stars which the old devil will drag along with his tail to make them perish. God will allow the old serpent to cause divisions among those who reign, in every society and every family. Physical and moral agonies will be suffered. God will abandon mankind to itself and will send punishments which will follow one after the other for more than thirty-five years."

"The society of men is on the eve of the most terrible scourges and the gravest events. Mankind must expect to be ruled with an iron rod and to drink from the chalice of wrath from God."

"May the vicar of my Son, Pope Pius IX never leave Rome again after 1859; may he, however, be steadfast and noble, may he fight with his weapons of faith and love. I will be at his side. May he be on his guard against Napoleon; he is two faced, and when he wishes to make himself Pope as well as Emperor, soon God will draw back from him. He is the eagle who, always wanting to rise higher, will fall on the sword he wished to use to force his people to be raised up."

"Italy will be punished for her ambition in wanting to shake off the yoke of the Lord of Lords. And so she will be left to fight a war; blood will flow on all sides. Churches will be locked up or desecrated. Priests and religious orders will be hunted down, and made to die a cruel death. Several will abandon the Faith and a great number of priests and members of religious orders will break away from the true religion; among these people there will even be bishops."

"May the Pope guard against the performers of miracles. For the time has come when the most astonishing wonders will take place in the earth and in the air."

"In the year 1864, Lucifer together with a large number of demons will be unloosed from hell; they will put an end to faith little by little, even in those dedicated to God. They will blind them in such a way, that unless they are blessed with a special grace, these people will take on the spirit of these angels in hell; several religious institutes will lose all faith and lose many souls."

"Evil books will be abundant on earth, and the spirit of darkness will spread everywhere, a universal slackening in all that concerns the service of God. They will have great power over Nature; there will be churches built to serve these spirits. People will be transported (spiritually) from one place to another by these evil spirits, even priests, for they will not have been guided by the good spirit of the gospel which is the spirit of humility, charity and zeal for the glory of God. On occasion, the dead and the righteous will be brought back to life."

(That is to say that these dead will take on the form of righteous souls which have lived on earth, in order to lead men further astray; these so-called resurrected dead, who will be nothing but the devil in this form, will preach another Gospel contrary to that of the true Jesus Christ, denying the existence of Heaven; that is to say, the souls of the damned. All these souls will appear as if united with their bodies.)

"In places there will be extraordinary wonders, because true faith has died and a false light shines on the world. Woe to the Princes of the Church whose only occupation will be to heap wealth upon more wealth, and to preserve their authority and proud domination!"

"The vicar of my Son will have much to suffer, as, for a time, the Church will be the victim of great prosecution: this will be a time of darkness. The Church will suffer a terrible crisis.

"As the holy Faith of God is forgotten, every individual will wish to be his own guide and superior to his fellow man. Civil and ecclesiastical authority will be abolished. All order and justice will be trampled underfoot. Nothing will be seen but murder, hatred, jealousy, falsehood and discord without love for the mother country or the family. The Holy Father will suffer greatly. I will be by His side to the end in order to receive his sacrifice. The wicked will make several attempts on his life, but they cannot harm Him. But neither he nor his successor will live to see the triumph of the Church of God.

"All the civil governments will have one and the same plan, which will be to abolish and do away with every religious principle, to make way for materialism, atheism, spiritualism and vices of all kinds.

"In the year 1865, there will be desecration of holy places. In convents, the flower of the Church will decompose and the devil will make himself like the King of all hearts. May those in charge of religious communities be on guard against the people they must receive, for the devil will resort to all his evil tricks to induce sinners into religious orders, for disorder and the love of carnal pleasures will be spread all over the earth.

"France, Italy, Spain and England will be at war. Blood will flow in the streets. Frenchmen will fight Frenchmen, Italian will fight Italian. A general war will follow which will be appalling. For a time, God will cease to remember France and Italy because the Gospel of Jesus Christ has been forgotten. The wicked will make use of all their evil ways. Men will kill each other, massacre each other even in their homes.

"At the first blow of His thundering sword, the mountains and all of Nature will tremble in terror, for the disorders and crimes of men have pierced the vault of the heavens. Paris will burn and Marseilles will be engulfed. People will believe that all is lost. Nothing will be seen but murder, nothing will be heard but the clash of arms and blasphemy.

"The righteous will suffer greatly. Their prayers, their penance and their tears will rise up to Heaven, and all of God's people will beg for forgiveness and mercy and will plead for my help and intercession. And then Jesus Christ, in an act of His justice and His great mercy will command His angels to have all His enemies put to death. Suddenly, the persecutors of the Church of Jesus Christ and all those given over to sin will perish and the earth will be desert-like. And then peace will be made, and man will be reconciled with God. Jesus Christ will be served, worshiped and glorified. Charity will flourish everywhere. The new kings will be the right arm of the Holy Church, which will be strong, humble, pious in its poor but fervent imitations of Jesus Christ. The Gospel will be preached everywhere and mankind will make great progress in its Faith, for their will be unity among the workers of Jesus Christ and man will live in fear of God.

"This peace among men will be short-lived. Twenty-five years of plentiful harvest will make them forget that the sins of men are the cause of all the troubles on this earth.

"A forerunner of the Antichrist, with his troops gathered from several nations will fight against the true Christ, the only Savior of the world. He will shed much blood and will want to annihilate the worship of God to make himself be looked upon as a God."

"The earth will be struck by calamities of all kinds (in addition to plague and famine which will be widespread). There will be a series of wars until the last war, which will then be fought by the ten kings of the Antichrist, all of whom will have one and the same plan and will be the only rulers of the world. Before this comes to pass, there will be a kind of false peace in the world. People will think of nothing but amusement. The wicked will give themselves over to all kinds of sin. But the children of the Holy Church, the children of the Faith, my true followers, they will grow in their love for God and in all the virtues most precious to Me. Blessed are the souls humbly guided by the Holy Spirit! I will fight on their side until they reach a fullness of years."

"Nature is asking for vengeance because of man, and she trembles with dread at what must happen to the earth stained with crime. Tremble, earth, and you who proclaim yourselves as serving Jesus Christ and who, on the inside only adore yourselves, tremble, for God will hand you over to His enemy, because the holy places are in a state of corruption. Many convents are no longer houses of God, but the grazing ground of Asmodeus and his like. It will be during this time that the Antichrist will be born of a Hebrew nun, a false virgin who will communicate with the old serpent, the master of impurity, his father will be a Bishop. At birth he will spew out blasphemy; he will have teeth, in a word, he will be the devil incarnate. He will scream horribly, he will perform wonders, he will feed on nothing but impurity. He will have brothers who, although not devils incarnate like him, will be children of evil. At the age of twelve they will draw attention to themselves by the gallant victories they have won; soon they will lead armies aided by the legions of hell.

"The seasons will be altered, the earth will produce nothing but bad fruit, the stars will lose their regular motion, the moon will reflect only a faint reddish glow. Water and fire will give the earth's globe convulsions and terrible earthquakes which will swallow up mountains, cities, etc....

"Rome will lose the faith and become the seat of the Antichrist.

"The demons of the air together with the Antichrist will perform great wonders on earth and in the atmosphere, and men will become more and more perverted. God will take care of his faithful servants and men of good will. The Gospel will be preached everywhere and people of all nations will get to know the truth.

"I make an appeal to the earth. I call on the true disciples of the living God who reigns in Heaven; I call on My children, the true faithful, those who have given themselves to Me so that I may lead them to My Divine

Son, those whom I carry in My arms, so to speak, those who have lived according to My spirit. Finally I call on the Apostles of the last Days, the faithful disciples of Jesus Christ who have lived in scorn for the world and for themselves, in poverty and humility, in scorn and in silence, in prayer and mortification, in chastity and in union with God, in suffering and unknown to the world. It is time they came out and filled the world with light. Go and reveals yourselves as My cherished children. I am on your side and within you, provided your faith is the light which shines upon you in these unhappy days. May your zeal make you hungry for the glory and the honor of Jesus Christ. Fight children of light, you, the few who can see. For now is the time of all times, the end of all ends.

"The Church will be in eclipse, the world will be in dismay. But now Enoch and Elijah will come, filled with the spirit of God. They will preach with the might of God, and men of goodwill will believe in God, and many souls will be comforted. They will make great strides forward through the virtue of the Holy Spirit, and will condemn the diabolic errors of the Antichrist. Woe to the inhabitants of the earth! There will be bloody wars and famines, plagues and infectious diseases. It will rain with a fearful hail of animals. There will be thunderstorms which will shake cities, earthquakes which will swallow up countries. Voices will be heard in the air. Men will beat their heads against walls, call for death, and on the other hand death will be their torment. Blood will flow on all sides. Who will be the victor if God does not shorten the duration of the test? At the blood, the tears and the prayers of the righteous, God will relent. Enoch and Elijah will be put to death. Pagan Rome will disappear. The fire of heaven will fall and consume three cities. All the universe will be struck with terror and many will let themselves be led astray because they have not worshiped the true Christ who lives among them. It is time; the sun is darkening; only faith will survive.

"Now is the time, the abyss is opening. Here is the king of kings of darkness, here is the Beast with his subjects, calling himself the Savior of the world. He will rise proudly in the air to go to Heaven. He will be smothered by the breath of the Archangel Saint Michael. He will fall, and the earth, which will have been in a continual series of evolutions for three days, will open up its fiery bowels; and he will be plunged for eternity with all his followers into the everlasting chasms of hell. And then water and fire will purge the earth and consume all the works of men's pride and all will be renewed. God will be served and glorified."

Miracles and Signs:

During interrogations from the local authorities, the children were taken to the site of the apparition. A man broke off a piece of rock at the spot of the Virgin's appearance and uncovered a spring. The spring was found to have healing powers which inspired the bishop to begin an official inquiry. Twenty-three cures were attributed to the mountain spring in the first year after the apparition.

Additionally, hundreds of miraculous cures have also been reported at the Basilica of La Salette.

Prophecies:

In December 1846, most of the popular crops were disease stricken, and in 1847 a famine hit Europe which resulted in the loss of approximately one million lives, including one hundred thousand in France alone.

Cholera became prevalent in various parts of France and claimed the lives of many children.

Description of the Virgin:

"The clothing of the Most Holy Virgin was silver white and quite brilliant. It was quite intangible. It was made up of light and glory, sparkling and dazzling. There is no expression nor comparison to be found on earth. The most Holy Virgin had a yellow pinafore.

"What am I saying, yellow? She had a pinafore more brilliant than several suns put together. It was not a tangible material; it was composed of glory, and the glory was scintillating, and ravishingly beautiful.

"The crown of roses which she placed on her head was so beautiful, so brilliant, that it defies imagination. The different colored roses were not of this earth; it was a joining together of flowers which crowned the Most Holy Virgin.

"The Most Holy Virgin was tall and well proportioned. She seemed so light that a mere breath could have stirred her, yet she was motionless and perfectly balanced. Her face was majestic, imposing. The voice of the Beautiful Lady was soft. It was enchanting, ravishing, warming to the ears.

"The eyes of the majestic Mary appeared thousands of times more beautiful than the rarest brilliants, diamonds, and precious stones. They shone like two suns; but they were soft, softness itself, as clear as a mirror.

"The Holy Virgin had a most pretty cross hanging around her neck.

"The Holy Virgin was crying nearly the whole time she was speaking to us. Her tears flowed gently, one by one, down to her knees, then, like sparks of light they disappeared. They were glittering and full of love. I would have liked to comfort her and stop her tears." - Melanie Mathieu (1851)

The Secret of La Salette:

The secret was given during the second stage of the apparition, when the Virgin Mary was standing upright and talked to the children. The secret has been written down in several versions and is the subject of much controversy.

There are at least eight preserved writings of the Secret of La Salette (3 by Maximin and 5 by Melanie) including the originals written in 1851 and the final version written in 1879. The final version has received the imprimatur of Salvatore Count Zola C.R.L., Bishop Zola of Lecce, Italy. There is one lost version written by Melanie in 1861.

In 1880 Pierre-Louis-Marie Cortet, bishop of Troyes, denounced the Lecce-imprimatured book to the Holy Office, and in turn Prospero Cardinal Caterini, secretary of the Congregation of the Holy Office, wrote back to him, to Vincenzo Maria Sarnelli, bishop of Castellammare di Stabia and to Pierre Archier M.S., superior general of the Missionaries of La Salette. The controversy ensues.

The two writings of July 1851 agree on the essential, but differ in their developments and even their tonality:

the secret of Maximin is shorter, simpler, and less serious. Mélanie is concerned to be understood by the recipient, and 'not to cause him too much sorrow', as she said, but this did not prevent the tears of Bishop de Bruillard.

Maximin initially wrote his Secret at the palace of Bishop de Bruillard on the evening of July 3, 1851. He was asked to rewrite it again because of spots of ink. The soiled autograph was burnt. The Bishop affixed his own seal to it and to send it to the pope. The sealed envelope was countersigned by two witnesses at 7:00 pm.

Melanie wrote the Secret a first time, on July 3, in Corenc, at the Sisters of Providence. She sealed it at 10:00 am, and it was carried at the Bishop's House. She chose to rewrite the secret on July 6 because she believed she misrepresented the chronology of events. After Melanie hand delivered the document, Bishop of Bruillard read the document before sealing it.

Below is the text of the secret as written for written for Pius IX in July 1851 and discovered by Fr. Michel Corteville in the Vatican Archives in October 1999. Please note that this is not the final version of the secret written in 1879.

The Secret of La Salette Written Statement by Maximin Giraud on July 3rd, 1851:

On September 19, 1846, we saw a beautiful Lady. We never said that this lady was the Blessed Virgin but we always said that it was a beautiful Lady.

I do not know if it is the Blessed Virgin or another person. As for me, I believe today that it is the Blessed Virgin. Here is what this Lady said to me:

"If my people continue, what I will say to you will arrive earlier, if it changes a little, it will be a little later.

France has corrupted the universe, one day it will be punished. The faith will die out in France: three quarters of France will not practice religion anymore, or almost no more, the other part will practice it without really practicing it. Then, after [that], nations will convert, the faith will be rekindled everywhere.

A great country, now Protestant, in the north of Europe, will be converted; by the support of this country all the other nations of the world will be converted.

Before all that arrives, great disorders will arrive, in the Church, and everywhere. Then, after [that], our Holy Father the Pope will be persecuted. His successor will be a pontiff that nobody expects.

Then, after [that], a great peace will come, but it will not last a long time. A monster will come to disturb it.

All that I tell you here will arrive in the other century, at the latest in the year two thousand."

Maximin Giraud
(She told me to say it sometime before.)
My Most Holy Father, your holy blessing to one of your sheep.
Grenoble, July 3, 1851.

The Secret of La Salette Written Statement by Melanie Mathieu on July 6th, 1851:

J.M.J.

secret which the Blessed Virgin gave me on the Mountain of La Salette on September 19, 1846 Secr[e]t.

Mélanie, I will say something to you which you will not say to anybody: The time of the God's wrath has arrived!

If, when you say to the people what I have said to you so far, and what I will still ask you to say, if, after that, they do not convert, (if they do not do penance, and they do not cease working on Sunday, and if they continue to blaspheme the Holy Name of God), in a word, if the face of the earth does not change, God will be avenged against the people ungrateful and slave of the demon.

My Son will make his power manifest! Paris, this city soiled by all kinds of crimes, will perish infallibly. Marseilles will be destroyed in a little time. When these things arrive, the disorder will be complete on the earth, the world will be given up to its impious passions.

The pope will be persecuted from all sides, they will shoot at him, they will want to put him to death, but no one will not be able to do it, the Vicar of God will triumph again this time.

The priests and the Sisters, and the true servants of my Son will be persecuted, and several will die for the faith of Jesus-Christ.

A famine will reign at the same time.

After all these will have arrived, many will recognize the hand of God on them, they will convert, and do penance for their sins.

A great king will go up on the throne, and will reign a few years. Religion will re-flourish and spread all over the world, and there will be a great abundance, the world, glad not to be lacking nothing, will fall again in its disorders, will give up God, and will be prone to its criminal passions.

[Among] God's ministers, and the Spouses of Jesus-Christ, there will be some who will go astray, and that will be the most terrible.

Lastly, hell will reign on earth. It will be then that the Antichrist will be born of a Sister, but woe to her! Many will believe in him, because he will claim to have come from heaven, woe to those who will believe in him!

That time is not far away, twice 50 years will not go by.

My child, you will not say what I have just said to you. (You will not say it to anybody, you will not say if you must say it one day, you will not say what that it concerns), finally you will say nothing anymore until I tell you to say it!

I pray to Our Holy Father the Pope to give me his holy blessing.

Mélanie Mathieu, Shepherdess of La Salette, Grenoble, July 6, 1851.

J.M.J.

Church Approval:

Mgr de Bruillard published a pastoral letter Sept 19, 1851 for the fifth anniversary of the Apparition in which he affirmed:

> "We judge that the Apparition of the Blessed Virgin to the two cowherds on the 19th of September, 1846, on a mountain of the chain of Alps, situated in the parish of LaSalette, in the archpresbytery of Corps, bears within Itself all the characteristics of truth, and that the faithful have grounds for believing it Indubitable and certain."

On November 4th, 1854, Mgr de Ginoulhiac issued a pastoral letter which condemned a memorandum published in Grenoble addressed to the Pope against the judgement of 1851. He additionally renews his predecessor's doctrinal judgement in a more explicit and this time definitive way.

Excerpts from The Pastoral Letter of Mgr de Bruillard, Bishop of Grenoble, on the Fifth Anniversary of the La Salette Apparition:

September 19, 1851 -"We judge that the Apparition of the Blessed Virgin to the two cowherds on the 19th of September, 1846, on a mountain of the chain of Alps, situated in the parish of LaSalette, in the archpresbytery of Corps, bears within Itself all the characteristics of truth, and that the faithful have grounds for believing it Indubitable and certain." (art. 1).

"Hence, in order to bear our warmest gratitude to God and to the glorious Virgin Mary, we authorise the devotion to Our Lady of La Salette. We allow the clergy to preach on this great Event and to draw the practical and moral consequences arising from it." (art. 3)

"We expressly forbid the faithful and the clergy of our diocese ever to speak or write against the Event which we proclaim this day and which, henceforth, demands the respect of all." (art. 5)

"We entreat you, our dear brethren, for the sake of your heavenly and even earthly interests, seriously to examine yourselves, to do penance for your sins, and particularly for those committed against the second and third commandments of God.) We entreat you, our dearly beloved brethren: make yourselves docile to the voice of Mary who calls you to penance, and who, on behalf of Her Son, threatens you with spiritual and temporal ills if, remaining insensitive to Her maternal warnings, you harden your hearts."

Declaration of Mgr Ginhoulhiac Concerning the La Salette Apparition:

September 19, 1855 —"The mission of the shepherds is ended; that of the Church begins. They can move away, become dispersed in the world, even unfaithful to the great grace received, but the Apparition of Mary will not thereby be shaken; for it is certain and nothing coming after can act against it."

Mgr Ginhoulhiac

Shrines:
- Official La Salette Shrine (France)
- National Shrine of Our Lady of La Salette (Attleboro, MA)
- La Salette Missionaries and Shrine of Twin Lakes, Wisconsin, (U.S.A)
- Shrine of Our Lady of La Salette -Enfield, NH
- The Shrine of Our Lady of La Salette-Altamont, New York

APPENDIX 5

OUR LADY OF FATIMA/ OUR LADY OF THE ROSARY: FATIMA, PORTUGAL (1917)

(Note: This appendix is taken directly from EWTN's The Miracle Hunter website (http://www.miraclehunter.com) which gives a succinct timeline and description of the apparition and messages.)

Summary:

While tending sheep in a field called Cova de Iria, Lucia de Santos (10) and her two cousins, Francisco and Jacinta Marto, reported six apparitions of Mary, who identified herself as "Our Lady of the Rosary." Mary urged prayer of the rosary, penance for the conversion of sinners and consecration of Russia to her Immaculate Heart.

Timeline:

3/22/1907	Lucia dos Santos was born on to Antonio and Maria Rosa dos Santos.
1908	Portugal's monarchy is overthrown
6/11/1908	Francisco Marto was born on to Manuel and Olimpia de Jesus Marto. He was the

	older brother of Jacinta and the first cousin of Lucia dos Santos.
3/11/1910	Jacinta Marto was born.
1911-1916	1,700 priests, nuns, and monks were killed by anti-Christian groups and public religious ceremonies were forbidden.
5/5/1917	Pope Benedict XV sends out pastoral letter to the world asking the faithful to petition Mary "that her most tender and benign solitude may be moved and the peace we ask for be obtained for our agitated world"
5/13/1917	Date of Eugenio Pacelli's (Pope Pius XII) Episcopal consecration.
5/13/1917	Three shepherd children, Lucia, Jacinta, & Francisco, see a ball of light near an oak tree and when they approach make out the light to be a beautiful lady. She says she is from Heaven and that she wishes the children to come to the Cova on the 13th of the month for 6 months.
6/13/1917	Our Lady appears for the second time to the children who came despite their parents' wishes for them to attend the St. Anthony Festival.
7/13/1917	The parish priest and Lucia's mother think the apparitions are diabolical but she decides to join the others at the Cova with 3,000 onlookers. They are told that a devotion to her Immaculate Heart would bring more souls to salvation. They are given three secrets: a vision of Hell, the consecration of Russia, and a papal assassination. Lucia

	turned pale and cried out with fear, calling Our Lady by name. There was a thunderclap, and the vision ended.
8/13/1917	The fourth apparition does not occur as planned due to the kidnapping of the children by an anti-Church civil administrator
8/19/1917	The children see Our Lady for the fourth time and she speaks of the need for penance for one's sins and those of the world.
9/13/1917	A crowd of thirty thousand witnesses the sun dim at noon and then a globe of light descending on the oak tree. White roses are seen falling from the sky and the visionaries are reminded of the importance of praying the rosary to end the war. They are told that St. Joseph and the child Jesus will accompany her at the October apparition.
10/13/1917	Our Lady appears to the children for the sixth time. She identified herself as "Our Lady of the Rosary" and the famous *dance of the sun* took place, witnessed by a crowd of 70,000 people. After the clouds of a rainstorm parted, numerous witnesses—some as far as 40 miles away—reported seeing the sun dance, spin, and send out colored rays of light
Oct 1918	Francisco and Jacinta became seriously ill with the Spanish flu which was part of an epidemic sweeping across the globe. It erupted in America and was spread by soldiers being sent to distant

THE COMING ERA OF PEACE

	lands. This epidemic killed an estimated twenty million people.
10/24-25/1917	The October revolution of Russia resulted in the creation of the Soviet government.
4/4/1919	Bed-ridden, Francisco requested his first Communion. The following day, Francisco died, April 14, 1919.
1919	Dom Jose Alves Correia da Silva, the Bishop of the Diocese of Leiria-Fatima, appointed a commission to study the case and began the official canonical inquiry.
2/20/1920	Jacinta Marto dies after suffering a long illness. She had been transferred to a Lisbon hospital and operated for an abscess in her chest, but her health did not improve.
10/13/1921	The first Mass at Cova da Iria was celebrated.
11/17/1921	A spring began to flow at the site of the apparitions.
1925	At age 18 Lucia became a postulant at the convent of the Dorothean Sisters at Pontevedra, Spain.
12/10/1925	At Pontevedra, Our Lady gave the young postulant nun the promise of the Five First Saturdays.
10/3/1928	Lucia pronounces her first vows.
10/13/1928	The foundation stone for the Basilica of Our Lady of the Rosary was laid.
6/13/1929	At Tuy, where, in the presence of the Holy Trinity, Mary further revealed to Lucia the spirit of this great devotion of

	reparation. "The moment has come in which God asks the Holy Father to make, in union with all the bishops of the world, the consecration of Russia to My Immaculate Heart, promising to save it by this means." (S. Zimdars-Schwartz, Encountering Mary, 197).
10/1/1930	The *Sacred Penitentiary* under Pius XI granted a partial indulgence to those who individually visited the Shrine and prayed for the intentions of the Holy Father, and a plenary indulgence once a month to those who went there in a group.
10/13/1930	Announcement of Dom Jose Alves Correia da Silva, Bishop of the Diocese of Leiria (now Leiria-Fatima) on the results of the Investigative Commission, declaring the apparitions "worthy of belief".
5/13/1931	The Portuguese bishops consecrated their nation to the Immaculate Heart
8/1931	Sister Lucia was staying with a friend at Rianjo, Spain to rest and recover while ill. In the chapel there, Our Lord complained to Sister Lucy of the tardiness of the Consecration of Russia to the Immaculate Heart of Mary
1935	Between 1935 and 1941, on the orders of her superiors, Sr. Lucia wrote four memoirs of the Fatima events. In the third of these, she recorded the first two parts of the secret, explaining that there was a third part she was not yet permitted by heaven to reveal. In the

	Fourth Memoir, she added a sentence to the end of the second part of the secret: "In Portugal, the dogma of the faith will always be preserved, etc." Sr. Lucia also noted that in writing the secret in the Fourth Memoir: "With the exception of that part of the Secret which I am not permitted to reveal at present, I shall say everything. I shall not knowingly omit anything, though I suppose I may forget just a few small details of minor importance." Upon the publication of the Third and Fourth Memoirs, the world became aware of the secret of Fatima and its three parts, including Our Lady's request that Russia be consecrated (entrusted) to her Immaculate Heart by the pope and the bishops of the world.
2/6/1938	Seven months before the declaration of war, Sister Lucy wrote to her bishop, Msgr. da Silva to tell him that war was imminent, but then spoke of a miraculous promise: "in this horrible war, Portugal would be spared because of the national consecration to the Immaculate Heart of Mary made by the bishops."
5/13/1938	The Portuguese bishops had vowed in 1936 that if Our Lady protected Portugal from the Communists, they would express their gratitude by renewing the National Consecration to the Immaculate Heart of Mary. True to their word, they renewed the

	Consecration of Portugal to the Immaculate Heart in thanksgiving for Our Lady's protection. Cardinal Cerejeira acknowledged publicly: "one cannot fail to recognize that the invisible hand of God has protected Portugal, sparing it the scourge of war and the leprosy of atheistic communism."
1940	Pope Pius XII spoke of Fatima for the first time in an official Papal text, his encyclical *Saeculo exeunte*, which was written to encourage the Church in Portugal to further its foreign missionary activity. In the text he stated: "Let the faithful not forget, especially when they recite the Rosary, so recommended by the Blessed Virgin Mary of Fatima, to ask the Virgin Mother of God to obtain missionary vocations, with abundant fruits for the greatest possible number of souls. ..."
1940	The Holy Father granted the new diocese of Nampula, in Mozambique, Our Lady of Fatima as its Patroness.
8/31/1941	Lucia reveals first two secrets in her writings in the "Third Memoir" for the Bishop of Leira-Fatima.
8/31/1942	In honor of the 25th Anniversary of the apparitions, Pope Pius XII (1939-1958) solemnly consecrated the world to the Immaculate Heart of Mary. On October 31, 1942, Pius XII consecrated not only Russia but the whole world to the Immaculate Heart of Mary. The world's

THE COMING ERA OF PEACE

	bishops were not involved.
1943	Sister Lucia explained that the Lord told her that He would accept this Act of Consecration to help speed the end of the World War II, but that it will not obtain worldwide peace. As predicted, this act obtained the end of the war, but did not usher in the reign of peace Our Lady promised, as it was not a consecration of specifically Russia, and the world's bishops did not participate in it. It was then placed in a wax-sealed envelope on which Sr. Lucia wrote that it should not be opened until 1960.
1946	Lucia entered the convent of the Carmelite Sisters of Coimbra under the name of Sister Maria Lucia of the Immaculate Heart.
9/1944	In 1943 Bishop da Silva suggested that Sister Lucy write down the text of the Third Secret and issues a formal order the following month at her request. She did not feel at liberty to do so until 1944.
1/2/1944	Sr. Lucia finally writes down the Third Secret after previously having claimed to have physically been unable to obey the command due to paralysis of a preternatural cause.
1/9/1944	Sr Lucia wrote to Bishop da Silva to tell him that the Third Secret had been written down and placed in a sealed envelope. Before giving the sealed envelope containing the third part of the "secret" to the then Bishop of Leiria-Fatima, Sister Lucia wrote on the

	outside envelope that it could be opened only after 1960, either by the Patriarch of Lisbon or the Bishop of Leiria [Bertone, MF, "Conversation with Sr. Maria Lucia"]. According to Sr. Lucia: "I fixed the date because I had the intuition that before 1960 it would not be understood, but that only later would it be understood. Now it can be better understood. I wrote down what I saw; however it was not for me to interpret it, but for the Pope" [ibid.]."
5/4/1944	The Holy See instituted the Feast of the Immaculate Heart of Mary
6/17/1944	The envelope was delivered to Bishop da Silva, by Sr Lucia's bishop confessor in Tuy. (The five month delay had resulted from Sister Lucia's unwillingness to entrust the envelope to anyone but a bishop.)
5/13/1946	Cardinal Masella, Papal Legate, crowned Our Lady of Fatima "Queen of the World" on the 300th Anniversary of the consecration of the nation of Portugal to Mary Immaculate. The entire Portuguese episcopate and over 600,000 pilgrims gathered at Fatima for the event.
10/13/1951	Pope's Legate, Cardinal Tedeschini, was sent to Fatima for the closing of the Holy Year. He told the crowd that Pope Pius XII had himself seen, repeated in Rome, the Miracle of the Sun that had occurred at the last Fatima apparition. The Holy Father had, in fact, been

	graced to see the Miracle of the Sun on four separate occasions the previous year: October 30 and 31, November 1, and November 8.
7/7/1952	Pope Pius XII consecrated Russia and her people to the Immaculate Heart. But he did the Consecration in a private ceremony, without inviting the world's bishops to join him, as Our Lady requested.
10/6/1953	The Basilica was solemnly consecrated by Cardinal Cerejeira, the Patriarch of Lisbon.
10/11/1954	Pope Pius XII issued an encyclical on the *Queenship of Mary*, and in it he referred to Her miraculous appearance at Fatima.
1956	The church on the apparition site was elevated to the rank of Basilica.
1957	The secret remained with the bishop of Leiria until 1957, when it was requested (along with photocopies of Sr. Lucia's other writings) by the Congregation for the Doctrine of the Faith. According to Cardinal Bertone the secret was read by both Pope John XXIII and Pope Paul VI. (see Message of Fatima, "Introduction".)
1964	At the closing ceremonies at the end of the third session of the Second Vatican Council, before all the Catholic bishops of the world, Pope Paul VI renewed Pius XII's consecration of the world to the Immaculate Heart of Mary. He also announced that a special envoy was to be sent to Fatima. In the Pope's name

	the Papal Legate would carry, as a symbolic gift, a Golden Rose to the Fatima Shrine. The inscription on it would say that Pope Paul was entrusting the entire Church to the care of Our Lady of Fatima.
5/13/1965	Pope Paul through his Papal Legate presented the Golden Rose at Fatima, commending the whole Church to Our Lady of Fatima's care.
5/13/1967	50th Anniversary of the apparitions, on May 13, 1967, Pope Paul VI went to Fatima on a pilgrimage of prayer and peace. On that occasion, he published an Apostolic Exhortation, *Signum Magnum*, in which he invited "all members of the Church to consecrate themselves to Mary Immaculate and to put this pious act into concrete action in their daily lives."
5/13/1981	A young Turk, Mehmet Alì Agca, shoots the Pope John Paul II in the abdomen and hand while he circles St. Peter's Square. "And thus we come to May 13, 1981, when I was wounded by gunshots fired in St. Peter's Square. At first, I did not pay attention to the fact that the assassination attempt had occurred on the exact anniversary of the day Mary appeared to the three children at Fatima in Portugal and spoke to them the words that now, at the end of this century, seem to be close to their fulfillment" (221). Read more: http://www.ncregister.com/blog/jimmy-akin/9-things-to-know-and-share-about-fatima/#ixzz2TDAOR58t

	Crossing the Threshold of Hope (1994)The pope later attributes being saved from the point blank assassination attempt to the intercession of Our Lady of Fatima: "It was a mother's hand that guided the bullet's path," he said, "and in his throes the Pope halted at the threshold of death" (*Meditation from the Policlinico Gemelli* to the Italian Bishops, May 13, 1994).
5/13/1982	Pope John Paul II offered Mass in Fatima to give thanks for Mary's intercession in saving his life a year earlier. He reminded the faithful that "the message of Fatima is a call to conversion and repentance, the nucleus of the message of the Gospel." He re-consecrated the world to Mary's Immaculate Heart and called all to prayer, especially the Rosary.
3/25/1984	Pope John Paul II consecrated the world to the Immaculate Heart of Mary in response to the request of Our Lady of Fatima" on 25 March 1984 in Saint Peter's Square, while recalling the fiat uttered by Mary at the Annunciation, the Holy Father, in spiritual union with the bishops of the world, who had been 'convoked' beforehand, entrusted all men and women and all peoples to the Immaculate Heart of Mary" (Bertone, Message of Fatima). "Sister Lucia personally confirmed that this solemn and universal act of consecration corresponded to what Our Lady wished ('Yes it has been done

	just as Our Lady asked, on 25 March 1984': Letter of 8 November 1989). Hence any further discussion or request is without basis" (Bertone, Message of Fatima).
5/13/2000	Pope John Paul II beatified the two deceased seers, Jacinta and Francisco. He has also made the Feast Day of Our Lady of Fatima universal by ordering it to be included in the Roman Missal. Francisco, 11, and Jacinta, 10, are the youngest non-martyrs to be beatified in the history of the Church.
6/26/2000	The third secret of Fatima is revealed by Pope John Paul II with Sr. Lucia in attendance.
11/17/2001	Sr. Lucia makes a statement to the secretary of the Congregation for the Doctrine of the Faith, Archbishop Tarcisio Bertone that the Fatima secret has been totally revealed by the Vatican, and Russia has already been consecrated as Mary requested.
2/21/2005	Lucia dos Santos dies at age 97.
2008	Pope Benedict XVI lifted the normal five-year waiting period to begin her canonization process.
5/12/2010	Benedict XVI's first stop upon arriving by helicopter to Fatima was to the Chapel of Apparitions to pray and to give Our Lady a Golden Rose. The Holy Father also noted that he brought with him a Golden Rose "as a homage of gratitude from the Pope for the marvels that the Almighty has worked through

	you in the hearts of so many who come as pilgrims to this your maternal home." Source: Zenit.org

Description of the Virgin:

"It was a lady dressed all in white, more brilliant than the sun, shedding rays of light clearer and stronger than a crystal glass filled with the most sparkling water and pierced by the burning rays of the sun."

Secret of Fatima:

Between 1935 and 1941, on the orders of her superiors, Sr. Lucia wrote four memoirs of the Fatima events. In the third of these, she recorded the first two parts of the secret, explaining that there was a third part she was not yet permitted by heaven to reveal. In the Fourth Memoir, she added a sentence to the end of the second part of the secret: "In Portugal, the dogma of the faith will always be preserved, etc." Sr. Lucia also noted that in writing the secret in the Fourth Memoir: "With the exception of that part of the Secret which I am not permitted to reveal at present, I shall say everything. I shall not knowingly omit anything, though I suppose I may forget just a few small details of minor importance." Upon the publication of the Third and Fourth Memoirs, the world became aware of the secret of Fatima and its three parts, including Our Lady's request that Russia be consecrated to her Immaculate Heart by the pope and the bishops of the world.

First Secret

The first part of the secret—the vision of hell—reveals to individuals the tragic consequences of failure to repent and what awaits them in the invisible world if they are not converted.

Second Secret

In the second part, Mary says: "You have seen hell where the souls of poor sinners go. To save them, God wishes to establish in the world devotion to my Immaculate Heart."

Cardinal Ratzinger explains: "According to Matthew 5:8, the 'Immaculate Heart' [of Mary] is a heart which, with God's grace, has come to perfect interior unity and therefore 'sees God.' To be 'devoted' to the Immaculate Heart of Mary means therefore to embrace this attitude of heart, which makes the fiat—'your will be done'—the defining center of one's whole life. It might be objected that we should not place a human being between ourselves and Christ. But then we remember that Paul did not hesitate to say to his communities: 'imitate me' (1 Cor. 4:16; Phil. 3:17; 1 Thess. 1:6; 2 Thess. 3:7, 9)" (op. cit.).

After explaining the vision of hell, Mary spoke of a war that "will break out during the pontificate of Pius XI." This latter war, of course, was World War II, which Sr. Lucia reckoned as having been occasioned by the annexation of Austria by Germany during the reign of Pius XI (J. de Marchi, Temoignages sur les apparitions de Fatima, 346). Our Lady also mentioned that this would happen after a night of the "unknown light." Sr. Lucia understood this to refer to January 25, 1938, when Europe was witness to a spectacular nighttime display of light in the sky. In her third memoir she wrote: "Your Excellency is not unaware that, a few years ago, God manifested that sign, which astronomers chose to call an aurora borealis.... God made use of this to make me understand that his justice was about to strike the guilty nations."

Our Lady added: "If my requests are heeded, Russia will be converted, and there will be peace; if not, she will spread her errors throughout the world, causing wars and persecutions of the Church. The good will be martyred; the Holy Father will have much to suffer; various nations will be annihilated. In the end, my Immaculate Heart will triumph. The Holy Father will consecrate Russia to me, and she shall be converted (*Portuguese: converterá - will change, i.e. become peaceful*) , and a period of peace will be granted to the world."

Third Secret

After the two parts which I have already explained, at the left of Our Lady and a little above, we saw an Angel with a flaming sword in his left hand; flashing, it gave out flames that looked as though they would set the world on fire; but they died out in contact with the splendor that Our Lady radiated towards him from her right hand: pointing to the earth with his right hand, the Angel cried out in a loud voice: 'Penance, Penance, Penance!'

And we saw in an immense light that is God: 'something similar to how people appear in a mirror when they pass in front of it' a Bishop dressed in White 'we had the impression that it was the holy father'.

Other Bishops, Priests, men and women Religious going up a steep mountain, at the top of which there was a big Cross of rough-hewn trunks as of a cork-tree with the bark; before reaching there the Holy Father passed through a big city half in ruins and half trembling with halting step, afflicted with pain and sorrow, he prayed for the souls of the corpses he met on his way; having reached the top of the mountain, on his knees at the foot of the big Cross he was killed by a group of soldiers who fired bullets and arrows at him, and in the same way there died one after another the other Bishops, Priests, men and women Religious, and various lay people of different ranks and positions.

Beneath the two arms of the Cross there were two Angels each with a crystal aspersorium in his hand, in which they gathered up the blood of the Martyrs and with it sprinkled the souls that were making their way to God [The Message of Fatima, "Third Part of the 'Secret'"].

In an interview at Fatima, Pope Benedict XVI (then Cardinal Joseph Ratzinger) spoke about visions and apparitions: "To all curious people, I would say I am certain that the Virgin does not engage in sensationalism; she does not act in order to instigate fear. She does not present apocalyptic visions, but guides people to her Son. And this is what is essential."

Third secret of Fatima is not, he said, "sensational or apocalyptic." He continued, "Preoccupation with the message and its presumed predictions of catastrophe are not part of a healthy Marian devotion. The Madonna did not appear to children, to the small, to the simple, to those unknown in the world in order to create a sensation." Mary's purpose "is, through these simple ones, to call the world back to simplicity, that is, to the essentials: conversion, prayer, and the sacraments."

From the Theological Commentary on Fatima from Cardinal Joseph Ratzinger (future Pope Benedict XVI): A careful reading of the text of the so-called third "secret" of Fatima, published here in its entirety long after the fact and by decision of the Holy Father, will probably prove disappointing or surprising after all the speculation it has stirred. No great mystery is revealed; nor is the future unveiled. We see the Church of the martyrs of the century which has just passed represented in a scene described in a language which is symbolic and not easy to decipher.... Thus we come finally to the third part of the "secret" of Fatima which for the first time is being published in its entirety [Ratzinger, MF, op. cit.].

Sr. Lucia herself indicated that she agreed with the interpretation offered by the Vatican: "Sister Lucia agreed with the interpretation that the third part of the "secret" was a prophetic vision, similar to those in sacred history. She repeated her conviction that the vision of Fatima concerns above all the struggle of atheistic Communism against the Church and against Christians, and describes the terrible sufferings of the victims of the faith in the twentieth century [Bertone, MF, op. cit.]."

Church Approval:

On October 13, 1930, Dom Jose Alves Correia da Silva, Bishop of the Diocese of Leiria-Fatima announced the results of the Investigative Commission, declaring the apparitions "worthy of belief."

October 1930 - Announcement of Dom Jose Alves Correia da Silva, Bishop of the Diocese of Leiria-Fatima on the Results of the Investigative Commission

In virtue of considerations made known, and others which for reason of brevity we omit; humbly invoking the Divine Spirit and placing ourselves under the protection of the most Holy Virgin, and after hearing the opinions of our Rev. Advisors in this diocese, we hereby:

1. Declare worthy of belief, the visions of the shepherd children in the Cova da Iria, parish of Fatima, in this diocese, from the 13th May to 13th October 1917.
2. Permit officially the cult of Our Lady of Fatima.

Every Pope since the apparitions has expressed approval of the supernatural character and stressed the importance of the messages of Fatima.

On May 13, 2000, Pope John Paul II beatified the two deceased seers, Jacinta and Francisco. He has also made the Feast Day of Our Lady of Fatima universal by ordering it to be included in the Roman Missal. In 2008, Pope Benedict XVI lifted the normal five-year waiting period to begin the canonization process of Sr. Lucia dos Santos.

In *Crossing the Threshold of Hope*, Pope John Paul II expressed his belief in Fatima this way: "And what are we to say of the three children from Fatima? ...They could not have invented these predictions. They did not know enough about history or geography, much less about social movements and ideological developments.

And nevertheless it happened just as they said."

The Feast of Our Lady of Fatima is May 13th.

Messages:

In these apparitions, Mary asked the children to pray the Rosary daily for the conversion of sinners and asked for devotion to her Immaculate Heart. She asked for prayer, penance and that Russia be consecrated to her Immaculate Heart. She also spoke of observing the first Saturdays of each month by going to confession and receiving Holy Communion to make reparation to the Hearts of Jesus and Mary.

MESSAGES OF AN ANGEL (1916):

Summer of 1916: The angel appeared again and said, "Pray, Pray a great deal. The Hearts of Jesus and Mary have merciful designs on you. Offer prayers and sacrifices continually to the Most High. Make everything you do a sacrifice, and offer it as an act of reparation for the sins by which God is offended, and as a petition for the conversion of sinners. Bring peace to our country in this way … I am the Guardian Angel of Portugal. Accept and bear with submission all the sufferings the Lord will send you."

Fall of 1916: The angel appeared to the children and prostrated himself on the ground before a vision of a chalice and host and said, "Most Holy Trinity, Father, Son and Holy Spirit, I adore Thee profoundly. I offer Thee the most precious Body, Blood, Soul and Divinity of Jesus Christ, present in all the Tabernacles of the world, in reparation for the outrages, sacrileges and indifferences whereby He is offended. And through the infinite merits of His most Sacred Heart and the Immaculate Heart of Mary, I beg of Thee the conversion of poor sinners."

MESSAGES OF OUR LADY (1917):

Sunday, May 13, 1917

Our Lady:	"Do not be afraid. I will do you no harm."
Lucia:	"Where are you from?"
Our Lady:	"I am from Heaven."
Lucia:	"What do you want of us?"
Our Lady:	"I came to ask you to come here on the thirteenth day for six months at this same time, and then I will tell you who I am and what I want. And afterwards, I will return here a seventh time."
Lucia:	"Will I go to Heaven?"
Our Lady:	"Yes, you will."
Lucia:	"And Jacinta?"
Our Lady:	"She also."
Lucia:	"And Francisco? Will he go to Heaven too?"
Our Lady:	"Yes, but first he must say many rosaries."
Our Lady:	"Would you like to offer yourselves to God to accept all the sufferings which He may send to you in reparation for the countless sins by which He is offended and in supplication for the conversion of sinners?

Lucia:	"Yes."
Our Lady:	"Then you will have much to suffer, but the grace of God will be your comfort."
All Three:	"O Most Holy Trinity I adore Thee. My God, my God, I love Thee in the Most Blessed Sacrament."

Wednesday, June 13, 1917

Lucia:	"My Lady, what do you want of me?"
Our Lady:	"I want you to come on the thirteenth day of next month and to pray the Rosary every day and I want you to learn to read."
Lucia:	(Lucia asked for the cure of a sick person.)
Our Lady:	"If she is converted, she will be cured within a year."
Lucia:	"I want you to take us to Heaven."
Our Lady:	"Yes, I will take Francisco and Jacinta soon, but you must remain on earth for some time. Jesus wishes to use you to make me better known and loved. He wishes to establish in the world devotion to my Immaculate Heart."
Lucia:	"Must I stay here all alone?"
Our Lady:	"No, my child, and would that make you suffer? Do not be disheartened. My Immaculate Heart will never abandon you, but will be your refuge and the way that will lead you to God."

Saturday, July 13. 1917

Lucia:	"What do you want of me?"
Our Lady:	"I want you to come on the thirteenth day of next month and to continue to pray the Rosary every day in honor of Our Lady of the Rosary, in order to obtain peace for the world and the end of the war for she alone can help."
Lucia:	"I would like to ask who you are and to perform a miracle so that people will believe that you are appearing to us."
Our Lady:	"Continue to come here every month. In October I will tell you who I am and what I want. And I will perform a miracle so that everyone may see and believe."
Lucia:	(Lucia then submitted petitions and prayer requests for Our Lady to present to God)
Our Lady:	(Our Lady gave some responses to Lucia)
Lucia:	"Yes, she wants people to recite the Rosary. People must recite the Rosary."
Our Lady:	"Sacrifice yourselves for sinners and say often, especially when you make some sacrifice, 'O my Jesus, this is for love of You, for the conversion of sinners, and in reparation for the offenses committed against the Immaculate Heart of Mary.' "
	(At this point the children see a terrifying vision of Hell.)
Our Lady:	"You saw Hell where the souls of poor sinners go. In order to save them, God

wishes to establish in the world devotion to my Immaculate Heart. If people do what I ask, many souls will be saved and there will be peace.

"The war is going to end. But if people do not stop offending God, another, even worse one will begin in the reign of Pius XI. When you shall see a night illuminated by an unknown light know that this is the great sign that God gives you that He is going to punish the world for its many crimes by means of war, hunger, and persecution of the Church and the Holy Father. To prevent it, I shall come to ask for the consecration of Russia to my Immaculate Heart and the Communion of reparation on the first Saturdays.

"If people attend to my requests, Russia will be converted and the world will have peace. If not, she [Russia] will scatter her errors throughout the world, provoking wars and persecutions of the Church. The good will be martyred, the Holy Father will have much to suffer, and various nations will be destroyed.

"In the end my Immaculate Heart will triumph. The Holy Father will consecrate Russia to me; it will be converted, and a certain period of peace will be granted to the world. In Portugal the dogmas of the Faith will always be kept"

	[At this point Lucia and Jacinta are given the Third Secret that was eventually given to the Pope]. "Do not tell this to anyone. Francisco ... yes, you may tell him" [Lucia and Jacinta both saw and heard Our Lady but Francisco only saw the apparitions]. "When you say the Rosary, say after each mystery: O my Jesus, forgive us our sins, save us from the fires of Hell and lead all souls to Heaven, especially those most in need."
Lucia:	"Do you want anything more of me?"
Our Lady:	"No, today I want nothing else of you."
Lucia:	"There she goes! There she goes!. Now you can't see her anymore."

Monday, August 13, 1917

The children received no messages on this day because they were detained by the authorities. Crowds who came to be with the children made claims of a soft light and fragrances in the area where Our Lady had appeared previously.

Sunday, August 19, 1917

Our Lady:	"Pray, pray a great deal and make many sacrifices for many souls go to Hell because they have no one to make sacrifices and to pray for them." "St. Joseph too will come with the Holy Child to bring peace to the world. Our

| | Lord will also come to bless the people. Our Lady of the Rosary and Our Lady of Sorrows will come too." |

Thursday, September 13, 1917

Lucia:	"You must pray!" "What do you want of me?"
Our Lady:	"Continue to pray the Rosary every day in order to obtain the end of the war. In October, Our Lord will come, and Our Lady of Sorrows and of Mount Carmel and St. Joseph with the Child Jesus to bless the world. God is pleased with your sacrifices, but He does not want you to sleep with the rope on; wear it only during the day."
Lucia:	"People have begged me to ask you many things. The cure of some sick persons, of a deaf mute ..."
Our Lady:	"Some I will cure, others not. In October I shall perform a miracle so that everyone may believe."
Lucia:	"If you wish to see her look in that direction."

Saturday, October 13, 1917

Lucia:	"Put down your umbrellas everyone!" "Kneel down. Our Lady is coming! I have seen the flash!" "What do you want of me?"
Our Lady:	"I am the Lady of the Rosary, I have come to warn the faithful to amend their lives and ask for pardon for their sins. They must not offend Our Lord anymore, for He is already too

	grievously offended by the sins of men. People must say the Rosary. Let them continue saying it every day." "I would like a chapel built here in my honor." "The war will end soon."
Lucia:	"Look at the sun!" [The rain had stopped and the black clouds parted and the sun began to whirl in the sky, scattering rays of multicolored light and lighting up the entire countryside. The sun whirled for three minutes, stopped and, then, resumed again a second and third time lasting a total of twelve minutes. The sun spun faster each time and at the end seemed to tear itself from the sky and began plunging to earth. The crowd was on their knees, terrified, asking pardon for their sins fearing that the end of the world was at hand. At the last moment the sun halted its descent and returned to its normal position. The miracle ended with the rain soaked earth and people's clothes now being completely dry. There were many reported healings. The miracle was seen over a 600 square mile area. The Portugal newspaper reporters gave long and detailed accounts but newspapers in most other countries ignored the story. As the crowd was witnessing the miracle of the sun, the children saw visions of the Holy Family, Jesus,

	Joseph and Mary. They also saw Our Lord carrying His cross with His Mother, Our Lady of Sorrows. Lucia also saw Our Lady of Mount Carmel who signifies the triumph over suffering.]

ADDITIONAL VISIONS OF JACINTA (1919-1920)

Our Lady:	"The sins of the world are very great ... If men only knew what eternity is, they would do everything in their power to change their lives." "You must pray much for sinners and priests and religious." "Priests must be pure, very pure. They should not busy themselves with anything except what concerns the Church and souls. The disobedience of priests and religious to their superiors and to the Holy Father gravely displeases Our Lord." "Fly from riches and luxury; love poverty and silence; have charity, even for bad people." "More souls go to Hell because of sins of the flesh than for any other reason." "Certain fashions will be introduced that will offend Our Lord very much."

"The Mother of God wants more virgin souls bound by the vow of chastity."

"Woe to women wanting in modesty."
"Confession is a sacrament of mercy and we must confess with joy and trust."

"Many marriages are not of God and do not please Our Lord."

"Let men avoid greed, lies, envy, blasphemy, impurity."

"Never speak ill of anyone. Never complain or murmur. Be very patient, for patience leads us to Heaven."

"Our Lady can no longer uphold the arm of her Divine Son which will strike the world. If people amend their lives, Our Lord will even now save the world, but if they do not, punishment will come."

"If the government of a country leaves the Church in peace and gives liberty to our Holy Religion, it will be blessed by God."

"Tell everybody that God gives graces through the Immaculate Heart of Mary. Tell them to ask graces from her, and that the Heart of Jesus wishes to be venerated together with the

| | Immaculate Heart of Mary. Ask them to plead for peace from the Immaculate Heart of Mary, for the Lord has confided the peace of the world to her." |

ADDITIONAL VISIONS OF LUCIA

December 10, 1925

Christ Child:	"Have compassion on the heart of your Most Holy Mother, covered with thorns, with which ungrateful men pierce it at every moment, and there is no one to make an act of reparation to remove them."
Our Lady	"Look my daughter, at my Heart, surrounded with thorns with which ungrateful men pierce me at every moment by their blasphemies and ingratitude. You at least try to console me and say that I promise to assist at the hour of death, with the graces necessary for salvation, all those who, on the first Saturday of five consecutive months, shall confess, receive Holy Communion, recite five decades of the Rosary, and keep me company for fifteen minutes while meditating on the fifteen mysteries of the Rosary, with the intention of making reparation to me."
Christ Child:	"And have you spread through the world what our heavenly Mother requested of you?
Lucia:	"My Jesus, You know very well what

	my confessor said to me in the letter I read to You. He told me that it was necessary for this vision to be repeated, for further happenings to prove its credibility, and he added that Mother Superior, on her own, could do nothing to propagate this devotion."
Christ Child:	"It is true that your Superior alone can do nothing, but with My grace she can do all. It is enough that your confessor gives you permission and that your Superior speak of it, for it to be believed, even without people knowing to whom it has been revealed."
Lucia:	"But my confessor said in the letter that this devotion is not lacking in the world, because there are many souls who receive You on the First Saturdays, in honor of Our Lady and of the fifteen Mysteries of the Rosary."
Christ Child:	"It is true My daughter, that many souls begin the First Saturdays, but few finish them, and those who do complete them do so in order to receive the graces that are promised thereby. It would please Me more if they did Five with fervor and with the intention of making reparation to the Heart of your heavenly Mother, than if they did Fifteen, in a tepid and indifferent manner...." [Lucia placed before Jesus the difficulty that some people had about confessing on Saturdays, and asked that it might

	be valid to go to confession within eight days.]
	"Yes, and it could be longer still, provided that, when they receive Me, they are in the state of grace and have the intention of making reparation to the Immaculate Heart of Mary."
Lucia:	"My Jesus, what about those who forget to make this intention?"
Christ Child:	"They can do so at their next confession, taking advantage of the first opportunity to go to confession."

December 17, 1927

Jesus:	"My daughter, write what they... [her spiritual director] ... ask of you. Write also all that the most holy Virgin revealed to you in the Apparition in which she spoke of this devotion. As for the remainder of the Secret, continue to keep silence."

June 13, 1929

I had requested and obtained permission from my superiors and my confessor to make a holy hour from 11:00 p.m. to midnight, from Thursday to Friday of each week.

Finding myself alone one night, I knelt down near the Communion rail, in the middle of the chapel, to recite the prayers of the Angel, lying prostrate ... Feeling tired, I got up and continued to recite them with my arms in the form of a cross. The only light was that of the [sanctuary] lamp.

Suddenly, the whole chapel lit up with a supernatural light and on the altar appeared a cross of light which reached the ceiling. In a clearer light, on the upper part of the cross, could be seen the face of a man with His body to the waist, on His chest a dove, equally luminous; and nailed to the cross, the body of another man. A little below the waist [of Christ on the cross], suspended in the air, could be seen a Chalice and a large Host, onto which some drops of Blood were falling, which flowed from the face of the Crucified One and from the wound in His breast. Running down over the Host, these drops fell into the Chalice.

Under the right arm of the cross was Our Lady with Her Immaculate Heart in Her hand … (She appeared as Our Lady of Fatima, with Her Immaculate Heart in Her left hand, without sword or roses, but with a crown of thorns and flames) under the left arm [of the cross], in large letters, like crystalline water which flowed over the altar, forming these words: "Grace and Mercy". I understood that the mystery of the Most Holy Trinity was shown to me, and I received lights about this mystery which I am not permitted to reveal.

Our Lady:	"The moment has come in which God asks the Holy Father, in union with all the bishops of the world, to make the consecration of Russia to my Immaculate Heart, promising to save it by this means. There are so many souls whom the Justice of God condemns for sins committed against me, that I have come to ask reparation: sacrifice yourself for this intention and pray."

| Jesus: | "They did not wish to heed My request. Like the King of France, they will regret it and then do it, but it will be late. Russia will already have spread her errors throughout the world, provoking wars and persecutions against the Church. The Holy Father will have much to suffer." |

1933

Our Lord communicated to Lucia that He was displeased that His requests had not been attended to.

Lucia:	"Why would you not convert Russia without the Holy Father making the consecration?"
Jesus:	"Because I want My whole Church to acknowledge that consecration as a triumph of the Immaculate Heart of Mary so that it may extend its cult later on and put the devotion of the Immaculate Heart besides the devotion to My Sacred Heart."
Lucia:	"But my God, the Holy Father probably will not believe me unless You Yourself move him with a special inspiration."
Jesus:	"The Holy Father, pray much for the Holy Father. He will do it, but it will be late. Nevertheless, the Immaculate Heart of Mary will save Russia. It has been entrusted to her."

Appendix 6

Our Lady of Akita: Akita, Japan (1973)

(Note: This appendix is taken directly from EWTN's The Miracle Hunter website (http://www.miraclehunter.com) which gives a succinct timeline and description of the apparition and messages.)

Summary:

Sister Agnes Sasagawa of the Handmaids of the Eucharist received visions of an angel and messages emanating from a wooden statue that wept 101 times.

1930	Agnes Sasagawa is born.
1946	The institute of Handmaids of the Eucharist was founded after Sumako Sugawara settled in the city in 1946.
5/12/1973	Agnes enters the convent of the Institute of the Handmaids of the Eucharist in Akita, Japan.
6/12/1973	Sr. Agnes encounters on several occasions a bright light emanating from the tabernacle in the chapel and "spiritual beings" worshipping the Eucharist. She reports these experiences to Bishop John Ito.

6/1973	Sr. Agnes begins to experience the stigmata. On Thursdays she feels initial pain and on Fridays and Saturdays finds a cross of blood on her left hand.
7/6/1973	Sr. Agnes encounters her guardian angel and subsequently a three-foot high wooden statue of the Virgin (Our Lady of All Nations) ablaze with light. The statue was created in 1963 by Saburo Wakasa, a sculptor based in Akita. The statue spoke to Agnes and asked her to pray for the reparation of the sins of humanity and to follow her superior. After the apparition, Agnes and the other nuns discover a bleeding wound in the hand of the statue.
7/26/1973	The angel appears again and promises that the pain in her wound would subside.
8/3/1973	The statue speaks again and warns of a great chastisement.
8/29/1973	The statue stops bleeding but tears start flowing down its cheeks. More than 2,000 people have since witnessed the statue weeping.
10/13/1973	Sr. Agnes receives her last message from the Virgin. She was told that the Father would inflict a terrible punishment on humanity, that fire would fall from the sky and wipe out part of the population, and that the devil would infiltrate the Church.
5/1974	The angel tells Agnes that her hearing

	will be temporarily restored and then permanently cured later.
10/13/1974	Agnes temporarily regains her hearing.
1/1975	The tears, sweat and blood from the statue were sent for laboratory analysis.
12/1975	The angel appears again.
1975	Bishop John Shojiro Ito (1962-1985) of Niigata went to Rome to the Sacred Congregation for the Doctrine of the Faith in 1975 where he consulted Archbishop Hamer, deputy secretary of this Congregation. He explained to the bishop that judgment regarding such a matter falls under the jurisdiction of the local Ordinary (bishop) of the diocese in question.
1976	Bishop Ito requested that the archbishop of Tokyo name the first commission of inquiry. (This first commission later declared that it was not in a position to prove the supernatural events of Akita.)
1976	Bishop Ito publicly announced that it was necessary to abstain from all official pilgrimage and all particular veneration of this statue while the inquiry was underway.
9/15/1981	The statue weeps for the 101st and last time
9/28/1981	Her guardian angel shows her a vision of the Bible and asks her to read Genesis 3:15: "I will place enmity between thee (Satan) and the woman

	(Mary), between thy seed and hers. She will crush thy head and thou shalt lie in wait for her heel."
8/4/1981	Theresa Chun is cured of a brain tumor after praying to our Lady of Akita.
5/30/1982	Agnes' hearing is restored permanently in accord with the promise of the angel.
4/22/1984	Approved by Bishop John Shojiro Ito of Niigata in a pastoral letter.
3/9/1985	Bishop Ito retires.
6/1988	Bishop Ito brought his letter to Joseph Cardinal Ratzinger -- now Pope Benedict XVI -- who allowed the pastoral letter and its dissemination to the faithful.
4/1990	The apostolic nuncio in Japan, Bishop William Aquin Carew in an interview with 30 DAYS, a Catholic Magazine, noted of Cardinal Ratzinger that: "His Eminence did not give any judgment on the reliability or credibility of the 'messages of the Virgin.' According to the transcription of the meeting, he simply affirmed that 'there are no objections to the conclusions of the pastoral letter.'"
7/1990	The president of the Japanese bishops' conference, Peter Seiichi Shirayanagi, told 30 DAYS," that, "The events of Akita are no longer to be taken seriously. We think they do not now have a great significance for the Church and Japanese society." (30

	DAYS Magazine, July - August 1990, "The Tears of Akita," by Stefano M. Paci, p. 45).
3/14/1993	Bishop Ito dies.
12/1999	The Apostolic Nuncio in Tokyo, Ambrose de Paoli, in response to a query from the editor of a British Catholic magazine *Christian Order*, stated: "The Congregation for the Doctrine of the Faith has asked me to respond to your query re: Akita. ... The Holy See has never given any kind of approval to either the events or messages of Akita." (*Christian Order*, December 1999, p. 610.)
2002	The chapel building was rebuilt in the style of traditional Japanese wooden architecture by carpenters who work on temples.

Description of the Virgin:

In the events of Akita, there was no "apparition" of the Virgin. Agnes reported the appearance of her guardian angel but the messages attributed to Mary were said to emanate from a bleeding 3-foot high wooden statue. The wooden statue in the convent at Akita was carved by a Buddhist woodcarver from an identical image of The Lady of All Nations.

Messages:

The Virgin delivered messages three times in 1973 (July 6, August 3, and October 13). Her guardian angel appeared an additional four times.

"As for the content of the messages received, it is no way contrary to Catholic doctrine or to good morals. When one thinks of the actual state of the world, the warning seems to correspond to it in many points. The Congregation of the Doctrine for the Faith has given me directives in this sense that only the bishop of the diocese in question has the power to recognize an event of this kind."

Bishop John Shojiro Ito, the Diocesan Bishop of Niigata

Received by: Sister Agnes Sasagawa, Order of the Handmaids of the Eucharist

JULY 6, 1973:

Her Guardian Angel: "Be not afraid. Pray with fervor not only because of your sins, but in reparation for those of all people. The world today wounds the most Sacred Heart of Our Lord by its ingratitude's and injuries. The wounds of Mary are much deeper and more sorrowful than yours. Let us go to pray together in the chapel."

The Virgin Mary: "My daughter, my novice, you have obeyed me well in abandoning all to follow me. Is the infirmity of your ears painful? Your deafness will be healed, be sure. Does the wound of your hand cause you to suffer? Pray in reparation for the sins of men. Each person in this community is my irreplaceable daughter.

Do you say well the prayer of the Handmaids of the Eucharist? Then, let us pray it together."

"Most Sacred Heart of Jesus, truly present in Holy Eucharist, I consecrate my body and soul to be entirely one with Your Heart, being sacrificed at every instant on all the altars of the world and giving praise to the Father pleading for the coming of His Kingdom."

"Please receive this humble offering of myself. Use me as You will for the glory of the Father and the salvation of souls." "Most holy Mother of God, never let me be separated from Your Divine Son. Please defend and protect me as Your Special Child. Amen."

"Pray very much for the Pope, Bishops, and Priests. Since your Baptism you have always prayed faithfully for them. Continue to pray very much…very much. Tell your superior all that passed today and obey him in everything that he will tell you. He has asked that you pray with fervor."

JULY 26, 1973:

Her Guardian Angel: "Your sufferings will end today. Carefully engrave in the depth of your heart the thought of the blood of Mary. The blood shed by Mary has a profound meaning. This precious blood was shed to ask your conversion, to ask for peace, in reparation for the ingratitude and outrages against the Lord. As with devotion to the Sacred Heart, apply yourself to devotion to the Most Precious Blood. Pray in reparation for all men. Say to your superior that the blood is shed today for the last time. Your pain also ends today. Tell them what happened today. He will understand all immediately. And you, observe his directions."

AUGUST 3, 1973:

"My daughter, my novice, do you love the Lord? If you love the Lord, listen to what I have to say to you."

"It is very important…You will convey it to your superior."

"Many men in this world afflict the Lord. I desire souls to console Him to soften the anger of the Heavenly Father. I wish, with my Son, for souls who will repair by their suffering and their poverty for the sinners and ingrates."

"In order that the world might know His anger, the Heavenly Father is preparing to inflict a great chastisement on all mankind. With my Son I have intervened so many times to appease the wrath of the Father. I have prevented the coming of calamities by offering Him the sufferings of the Son on the Cross, His Precious Blood, and beloved souls who console Him forming a cohort of victim souls. Prayer, penance and courageous sacrifices can soften the Father's anger. I desire this also from your community…that it love poverty, that it sanctify itself and pray in reparation for the ingratitude and outrages of so many men.

Recite the prayer of the Handmaids of the Eucharist with awareness of its meaning; put it into practice; offer in reparation (whatever God may send) for sins. Let each one endeavor, according to capacity and position, to offer herself entirely to the Lord."

"Even in a secular institute prayer is necessary. Already souls who wish to pray are on the way to being gathered together. Without attaching to much attention to the form, be faithful and fervent in prayer to console the Master."

"Is what you think in your heart true? Are you truly decided to become the rejected stone? My novice, you who wish to belong without reserve to the Lord, to become the spouse worthy of the Spouse, make your vows knowing that you must be fastened to the Cross with three nails. These three nails are poverty, chastity, and obedience. Of the three, obedience is the foundation. In total abandon, let yourself be led by your superior. He will know how to understand you and to direct you."

OCTOBER 13, 1973:

"My dear daughter, listen well to what I have to say to you. You will inform your superior."

"As I told you, if men do not repent and better themselves, the Father will inflict a terrible punishment on all humanity. It will be a punishment greater than the deluge, such as one will never seen before. Fire will fall from the sky and will wipe out a great part of humanity, the good as well as the bad, sparing neither priests nor faithful. The survivors will find themselves so desolate that they will envy the dead. The only arms which will remain for you will be the Rosary and the Sign left by My Son. Each day recite the prayers of the Rosary. With the Rosary, pray for the Pope, the bishops and priests."

"The work of the devil will infiltrate even into the Church in such a way that one will see cardinals opposing cardinals, bishops against bishops. The priests who venerate me will be scorned and opposed by their confreres…churches and altars sacked; the Church will be full of those who accept compromises and the demon will press many priests and consecrated souls to leave the service of the Lord.

"The demon will be especially implacable against souls consecrated to God. The thought of the loss of so many souls is the cause of my sadness. If sins increase in number and gravity, there will be no longer pardon for them."

"With courage, speak to your superior. He will know how to encourage each one of you to pray and to accomplish works of reparation."

"It is Bishop Ito, who directs your community."

"You have still something to ask? Today is the last time that I will speak to you in living voice. From now on you will obey the one sent to you and your superior."

"Pray very much the prayers of the Rosary. I alone am able still to save you from the calamites which approach. Those who place their confidence in me will be saved."

DECEMBER 1975:

Her Guardian Angel: "Do not be surprised to see the Blessed Virgin weeping. She weeps because she wishes the conversion of the greatest number. She desires that souls be consecrated to Jesus.

SEPTEMBER 28, 1981:

Her Guardian Angel:

"There is a meaning to the figure 101 (the number of times the statue wept). This signifies that sin came into the world by a woman and it is also by a woman that salvation came into the world. The zero between the two signifies the Eternal God who is from all eternity until eternity. The first one represents Eve, and the last, the Virgin Mary."

Sources:

God-Sent: A History of the Accredited Apparitions of Mary
Roy Abraham Varghese
Crossroad Publishing Company
New York, NY 2000.

<u>Miracles, Cures, and Signs:</u>

The statue wept 101 times. Her guardian angel explained it with the following: "There is a meaning to the figure 101 (the number of times the statue wept). This signifies that sin came into the world by a woman and it is also by a woman that salvation came into the world. The zero between the two signifies the Eternal God who is from all eternity until eternity. The first one represents Eve, and the last, the Virgin Mary."

The actual weeping of the statue was not only witnessed by the local bishop but was shown on national Japanese TV.

Theresa Chun, a Korean woman diagnosed with a brain tumor, placed an image of Our Lady of Akita under her pillow and prayed to her for a miraculous healing. On August 4, 1981, the tumor was found to have disappeared. This healing was well documented by Fr. Joseph Oh of Seoul, S. Korea.

In May 1982, her angel told Agnes that her hearing would be permanently restored that month, and on May 30 the deafness was cured. (Tests performed on Agnes at the Akita Municipal Hospital in 1975 had confirmed that she was deaf and that her deafness was incurable.)

Approval:

The first tests on the samples of blood, tears, and sweat from the statue were performed by Professor Eiji Okuhara, a Catholic physician in the Akita University Department of Biochemistry and a former Rockefeller Foundation fellow. Professor Okuhara, who had witnessed the weeping statue himself, also passed the samples on to a non-Christian forensic specialist, Dr. Kaoru Sagisaka. The scientists confirmed that the samples were of human origin- the blood was found to be type B and the sweat and tears were type AB.

Initially the nun's claims were rejected by an archbishop, then accepted by the bishop of her actual diocese, Most Reverend John Shojiro Ito of Niigata, who on April 22, 1984, after years of extensive investigation, declared the tears to be of supernatural origin and authorized veneration of the Holy Mother of Akita.

"After the inquiries conducted up to the present day, one cannot deny the supernatural character of a series of unexplainable events relative to the statue of the Virgin honored at Akita (Diocese of Niigata). Consequently I authorize that all of the diocese entrusted to me venerate the Holy Mother of Akita."

Bishop John Shojiro Ito of Niigata (April 22, 1984)

Bishop Ito was apprehensive over the reaction of the Vatican to his pastoral letter, but when he brought his letter to Joseph Cardinal Ratzinger — now Pope Benedict XVI — in 1988, the cardinal, who was initially disinclined toward the revelation, allowed the pastoral letter and its dissemination to the faithful. The Vatican has never issued a formal statement.

Our Lady of Akita Shrine
"Redemptoris Mater"
The Chapel of Seitai Hoshikai
Handmaids of the Holy Eucharist
Soegawa Yuzawadai 1
Akita 010-0822 JAPAN

As of 2017, the shrine receives about 7,000 pilgrims a year, and I think about two-thirds of them are from overseas according to Keiko Ogawa, the Mother Superior.

The Motherhouse of the Institute of the Handmaids of the Sacred Heart of Jesus in the Holy Eucharist stands atop a hill away from residential homes. It is located about seven kilometers north of Akita Station, which takes about six hours to reach from Narita International Airport in Chiba Prefecture, a major gateway into Japan, using express and bullet trains.

APPENDIX 7

RECONCILER OF PEOPLE AND NATIONS: BETANIA, VENEZUELA (1976)

(Note: This appendix is taken directly from EWTN's The Miracle Hunter website (http://www.miraclehunter.com) which gives a succinct timeline and description of the apparition and messages.)

Summary:

Maria Esperanza of Betania, Venezuela has witnessed 31 apparitions of the Blessed Virgin Mary over the course of 15 years. The Virgin called herself the "Reconciler of People and Nations" and warned of impending war and suffering. Many visitors have come to the site, reporting numerous miracles and signs. On one occasion in 1984, 108 people claimed to have witnessed a public apparition of the Virgin.

The local bishop approved the authenticity of Maria's experiences in 1987.

Timeline:

Nov 22, 1928	Maria Esperanza Medrano de Bianchini is born in Betania, Venezuela.
1933	Maria has a vision of St. Theresa of Lisieux who gave her a rose.
1940	Maria nears death from bronchial pneumonia and receives a vision of Mary who recommends the appropriate medications.
	During her adolescence she was healed from a paralyzing illness after an apparition of the Sacred Heart of Jesus.
1950	Visits Padre Pio and promises her that "When I leave, she will be your consolation."
Oct 3, 1954	She subsequently enters a Franciscan convent for a brief period before being told that she did not have a vocation. St Therese appears to her and tells her that she is to be a wife and mother. She receives another vision from the Sacred heart of Jesus instructing her to go to Rome, where she meets her future husband, Geo Bianchini.
Dec 8, 1956	Maria marries Geo Bianchini on the Feast of the Immaculate Conception.
1974	Maria and Geo purchase a farm shown to her by Mary in a vision predicting that it would become a center of "constant prayer and pilgrimage" for all "the nations of

	the world". Mary introduces herself as "Reconciler of People and Nations".
March 25, 1976	First apparition of Mary at the grotto site.
March 25, 1984	108 people see the Virgin at the grotto as she first appears to the children at a waterfall and then to the adults of the group at Mass.
1984	Pío Bello Ricardo, S.J., Bishop of Los Teques opens an investigation.
Nov 21, 1987	Archbishop Pio Bello Ricardo emits the Pastoral Instruction on the apparition of Our Blessed Virgin Mary in Finca Betania, approving the apparitions received by Maria.
Jan 5, 1990	The Virgin appears for the last time (31) to Maria.
Dec 8, 1991	A eucharistic miracle was reported in which the Host began to bleed. Tests in Caracas later determined the blood to be human.
Aug 7, 2004	Maria Esperanza dies in New Jersey, USA.
Jan 31, 2010	Bishop Paul Bootkoski, Ordinary of the Diocese of Metuchen, New Jersey, opens her cause for beatification and canonization. (Since Maria Esperanza died in New Jersey, her cause is being initiated there.)

Description of the Virgin:

"And when she revealed herself, she went to the top of the tree, and I saw she was beautiful, with her hair brown, dark brown, her eyes that were light brown and she had very fine, very pretty eyebrows, tiny mouth, a nose very straight and her complexion was so beautiful, it was skin that seemed like silk. It was bronzed. It was beautiful. Very young. Her hair was down to here, to her shoulders." - Maria Esperanza

Messages:

The Virgin appeared 31 times between March 25, 1976, to January 5, 1990. Twenty-four of the apparitions came after 1984.

The messages that Our Lady of Betania brought is one of reconciliation and love:

"Behold, children, the love of a Mother, who cherishes you… and comes as a starting point to lead you toward a law of justice, love, peace, and reconciliation!

I call you, for the great moment of reconciliation has arrived…. I extend my love to all my children, dwellers on earth, and be loyal to Jesus, so may discover the wonderful secret of unity…which will help us find the key to God's kingdom!

…Forgive one another. Love one another. Serve one another… All of you are children of God. All are loved."

Miracles, Cures, and Signs

There have been over 500 miracles and cures reported at Betania. On December 8, 1991, a eucharistic miracle was reported in which the Host began to bleed. Tests in Caracas later determined the blood to be human.

Pilgrims have claimed to have seen the Virgin (over 2,000 testimonies) and various celestial phenomena such as mist coming from the hill, a profusion of flowers, the sound of an invisible choir, the scent of roses and the irregular movement of the sun.

Maria was the subject of many miraculous happenings including the stigmata and exuding sweet aromas. The eucharist has appeared in her mouth and she allegedly displayed gifts of healing, levitation, bilocation, and prophecy. One of the most remarkable phenomena is the rose that spontaneously bursts forth from her chest, having done so 16 times.

Approval:

The bishop of the diocese, Pío Bello Ricardo, S.J., Bishop of Los Teques, opened an investigation 1984. He interviewed witnesses and examined more than 500 cures attributed to Our Lady of Betania, among which was the cure of a baby's spina bifida, as documented in Westchester County Medical Center in Valhalla, New York.

November 21, 1987 —"After having studied repeatedly the apparitions of the Most Holy Virgin in Betania, and having begged the Lord earnestly for spiritual discernment, I declare that in my judgement the said apparitions are authentic and have a supernatural character. I therefore approve, officially, that the site where the apparitions have occurred be considered as sacred."

- Bishop Pio Bello Ricardo

Appendix 8

Our Lady of Cuapa: Cuapa, Nicaragua (1980)

(Note: This appendix is taken directly from EWTN's The Miracle Hunter website (http://www.miraclehunter.com) which gives a succinct timeline and description of the apparition and messages.)

Summary:

Church sacristan Bernardo Martinez entered an old chapel and observed a supernatural light illuminating from a statue of the Blessed Virgin. On another day, the Virgin appeared clothed in white (similar to the statue in the church) and asked for the daily Rosary with Biblical citations and have the First Saturday Devotions renewed. She also warned of future sufferings for Nicaragua if the people didn't change. Not wanting further problems, he ignored the Virgin's request to spread the message, and when he avoided the location of the apparition, the Virgin appeared to him a few days later in a pasture promising him help.

Timeline:

1880	Fr. Andres Rongier, SJ, a Jesuit missionary from Mexico, prophesied that Cuapa would be a famous future site of a Marian apparition.
8/20/1931	Bernardo Martinez is born
4/15/1980	Bernardo discovered that the statue in the chapel was supernaturally lighting up on its own
5/8/1980	The Virgin appeared clothed in white (similar to the statue in the church) and asked for the daily Rosary with Biblical citations and have the First Saturday Devotions renewed. She also warned of future sufferings for Nicaragua if the people didn't change. Not wanting further problems, he ignored the Virgin's request to spread the message.
5/16/1980	Not wanting further problems, he ignored the Virgin's request to spread the message, and when he avoided the location of the apparition, the Virgin appeared to him in a pasture promising him help. The next morning, an inner peace filled his soul which allowed him to tell what happened with no fear of ridicule.
6/8/1980	The Virgin gave him a nighttime vision (a 'movie in the sky') which moved from the early church to men in white (like Dominicans) praying the Rosary, then Franciscans, and finally ordinary people with Rosaries whose example he was told to follow.

7/8/1980	An Angel appeared and told him and foretold several events which shortly took place (including the death of a cousin which could have been prevented had he listened to Bernardo's warning.)
9/8/1980	The Virgin appeared as a child and told him to not raise funds for a new Church: "The Lord does not want material churches. He wants living temples which are yourselves."
10/13/1980	The Virgin Mary appeared in a big luminous circle forming over the ground and allowed everyone (50) there to witnessed. When her form appeared he pleaded with her to allow herself to be seen by the others for they didn't believe. Her face turned pale and her garments grey as she became visibly saddened by their hardness of heart. As Bernardo apologized profusely, she instructed him to pray the Rosary, turn from violence, pray for the world, and make peace. She tells him that he will no longer see her in that place and vanishes.
1982	Bishop Bosco M Vivas Robelo, Auxiliary Bishop and Vicar General of the Archdiocese of Managua, authorizes "the publication of the narration of the apparitions of the Blessed Virgin Mary in Cuapa."
11/13/1982	Pablo Antonio Vega Mantilla, Bishop of Juigalpa (the diocese of the apparitions) declares that he has "an

| | obligation to assure the authenticity of the events in order to be able to assist in discerning the true value of the alluded to message." |
| | Bernardo Martinez is ordained a priest |

<u>Description of the Virgin:</u>

"Suddenly I saw a lightning flash. I thought and said to myself, 'It is going to rain.' But I became filled with wonder because I did not see from where the lightning had come. I stopped but I could see nothing - no signs of rain. Afterward I went over near a place where there are some rocks. I walked about six or seven steps. That was when I saw another lightning flash, but that was to open my vision, and she presented herself.

"I was then wondering whether this could be something bad, whether it was the same statue as in the chapel. But I saw that she blinked and that she was beautiful. She remained above the pile of rocks as if on a cloud. And there was a little tree on top of the rocks and over that tree was the cloud. The cloud was extremely white. It radiated in all directions the ray of sun light. On the cloud were the feet of a very beautiful lady. Her feet were bare. The dress was long and white with a celestial cord around the waist, and it had long sleeves. Covering her was a veil, a pale cream color, with gold embroidery along the edge. Her hands were held together over her breast. It looked like the statue of the Virgin of Fatima."

- Bernardo Martinez

Messages:

The Virgin asked for the daily Rosary with Biblical citations and have the First Saturday Devotions renewed. She also warned of future sufferings for Nicaragua if the people didn't change.

After the initial four apparitions, the Virgin reportedly subsequently appeared in later years with messages of the destruction of atheistic communism and the whole world. She also requested the propagation of the devotion to the shoulder wounds of Christ.

"I come from heaven. I am the Mother of Jesus... I want the Rosary to be prayed every day... I want it to be prayed permanently within the family... including the children old enough to understand... to be prayed at a set hour when there are no problems with the work in the home."

She told me that the Lord does not like prayers we make in a rush or mechanically. Because of that she recommended praying of the Rosary with the reading of Biblical citations that we put into practice the Word of God.

"Love each other. Comply with your obligations. Make peace. Don't ask our Lord for peace because if you do not make it there will be no peace."

"Renew the first five Saturdays. You received many graces when all of you did this." *"Nicaragua has suffered much since the earthquake. She is threatened with even more suffering. She will continue to suffer if you don't change. Pray, pray, my son, the Rosary for all the world. Tell believers and non-believers that the world is threatened by grave dangers. I asked the Lord to appease*

his justice, but if you don't change you will hasten the arrival of the Third World War."

I ... talked to her about the church that the people wanted to build in her honor. Fr. Domingo told us that this was a decision he could not make and that we should tell it to the Holy Virgin. That is why I presented this question to her. Because a man from Matagalpa had already given us C$80.00 cordobas to this end. She answered me saying, '*No, the Lord does not want material churches. He wants living temples which are yourselves. Restore the sacred temple of the Lord. In you is the gratification for the Lord.' 'Love each other. Love one another. Forgive each other. Make peace. Don't ask for it. Make peace!' 'From this day on do not accept even one cent for anything.'*

When she had finished giving her message I remembered the requests from the people of Cuapa... *"They ask of me things that are unimportant. Ask for faith in order to have the strength so that each can carry his own cross. The sufferings of this world cannot be removed. Sufferings are the cross which you must carry. That is the way life is. There are problems with the husband, with the wife, with the children, with the brothers. Talk, converse, so that problems will be resolved in peace. Do not turn to violence. Never turn to violence. Pray for faith in order that you will have patience."*

"Do not be grieved. I am with all of you even though you do not see me. I am the mother of all of you, sinners. Love one another. Forgive each other. Make peace because if you don't make it, there will be no peace. Do not turn to violence. Never turn to violence. Nicaragua has suffered a great deal since the earthquake and will

continue to suffer if all of you don't change. If you don't change you will hasten the coming of the third world war. Pray. Pray, my son, for all the world. A mother never forgets her children. And I have not forgotten what you suffer. I am the mother of all of you, sinners."

Approval:

In 1982, both Bishop Bosco M. Vivas Robelo, Auxiliary Bishop and Vicar General of the Archdiocese of Managua and Bishop Pablo Antonio Vega M., Prelate Bishop of Juigalpa (the diocese where the apparitions took place) released statements positively affirming the apparitions.

Declaration of Bishop Bosco M. Vivas Robelo, Auxiliary Bishop and Vicar General of the Archdiocese of Managua

1982 — "I, the undersigned, Auxiliary Bishop and Vicar General of the Archdiocese of Managua, authorize the publication of the narration of the apparitions of the Blessed Virgin Mary in Cuapa."

Source: Varghese, Roy Abraham . *God-Sent: A History of the Accredited Apparitions of Mary.*Crossroad Publishing Company. New York 2000.

Statement of Bishop Pablo Antonio Vega M., Prelate Bishop of Juigalpa

November 13, 1982 — "It has been nearly three years now since one of the peasants from the area arrived communicating a message which he said he received from Mary in a series of dreams and apparitions… Because of the duty and obligation to protect the wholesome piety of the faithful and for the truth of those events, in my capacity as bishop of the area, I find an obligation to assure the authenticity of the events in order to be able to assist in discerning the true value of the alluded to message... The 'report' that we present retains the accurate content and language used by the individual who received the visions."

Source:

Information cited from Dictionnaire Des Apparitions De La Vierge Marie by Rene Laurentin and Patrick Sbalchiero, Fayard, 2007.

Varghese, Roy Abraham . *God-Sent: A History of the Accredited Apparitions of Mary.*Crossroad Publishing Company. New York 2000.

<u>Statement of Bishop Robelo of Leon (June 10, 1994):</u>

Bishop Robelo of Leon provided the following authorization of the accounts of the apparitions entitled *Let Heaven and Earth Unite!* compiled by Stephen and Miriam Weglian: "I hereby authorize the publication of the story of the Apparitions of the Blessed Virgin Mary in Cuapa and the messages given to Bernardo Martinez under the title Let Heaven and Earth Unite! May this publication help those who read it to have an encounter with Jesus Christ in the Church through the mediation of the Mother of Our Lord."

Source:

Dictionnaire Des Apparitions De La Vierge Marie by Rene Laurentin and Patrick Sbalchiero, Fayard, 2007.

Varghese, Roy Abraham . God-Sent: A History of the Accredited Apparitions of Mary.Crossroad Publishing Company. New York 2000.

Appendix 9

NYINA WA JAMBO (MOTHER OF THE WORD): KIBEHO, RWANDA (1981)

(Note: This appendix is taken directly from EWTN's The Miracle Hunter website (http://www.miraclehunter.com) which gives a succinct timeline and description of the apparition and messages.)

Summary:

The apparitions began in November 1981 when six young girls and one boy claimed to see the Blessed Virgin Mary and Jesus. But only the visions of the first three – 17-year-old Alphonsine, 20-year-old Nathalie, and 21-year-old Marie Claire – have received Bishop Misago's solemn approval. Because there were reservations about the other four visionaries, and the supposed visions of Jesus, Bishop Misago didn't confirm the authenticity of either those visions or visionaries.

The Virgin appeared to them with the name "Nyina wa Jambo", that is "Mother of the Word," which is synonymous to "Umubyeyl W'iamna" that is, "Mother of God," as she herself explained.

Timeline:

Nov 28, 1981	At 12:35 p.m. in the school dining room, Alphonsine Mumureke heard a voice calling her: "My daughter." (Alphonsine was at a boarding school run by nuns, which the girl and the other two approved visionaries were attending.) Mumureke asked her: "Who are you?" The reply was: "Ndi Nyina Wa Jambo," that is, "I am the Mother of the Word." She continued: "I have come to calm you because I have heard your prayers. I would like your friends to have faith, because they do not believe strongly enough."
Jan 1982	Our Lady begins appearing to Nathalie Mukamazimpaka for nearly two years.
March 2, 1982	Our Lady begins appearing to Marie Claire Mukangango for 6 months.
Sept 15, 1982	The last of Marie Claire's visions
1982	Bishop Jean Baptiste Gahamanyi appoints a medical commission, and later a theological one, to investigate the reports. He then authorized public devotion.
Dec. 3, 1983	The last of Nathalie's visions
Aug. 15, 1988	The local Bishop approved a public devotion linked to the apparitions of Kibeho.

Nov. 28, 1989	The last of Alphonsine's visions -- exactly eight years since the first.
1990	John Paul II visits Rwanda and exhorts the faithful to turn to the Virgin as a simple and sure guide, and pray for greater commitment against local divisions, both political and ethnic.
Nov 28, 1992	Construction begins on Marian sanctuary called "Shrine of Our Lady of Sorrows"
1994	The vision is now considered a prophecy of the ethnic genocide that would take place in the country 13 years later. Tragically, in 1994, visionary Marie Claire became one of its victims.
June 29, 2001	On the solemnity of Sts Peter and Paul, during a solemn Mass concelebrated in the cathedral of Gikongoro, Bishop Augustin Misago presented his declaration on authenticity of the apparitions.
July 2, 2001	The Holy See released the declaration of Bishop Augustin Misago of Gikongoro approving the apparitions. Declared valid were the apparitions to three visionaries: Alphonsine Mumureke, Nathalie Mukamazimpaka and Marie Claire Mukangango.
2003	Cardinal Crescenzio Sepe,

	prefect of the Congregation for the Evangelization of Peoples, consecrated the Marian shrine dedicated to Our Lady of Sorrows in the site of the apparitions in Kibeho. He expressed the hope that Kibeho would become a place in which a Rwandan people would be born renewed in faith and forgiveness. (Source: Zenit.org)
Sept 8, 2006	Bishop Augustine Misago of Gikongoro announced that the celebrations for the 25th anniversary would begin on Nov. 28, feast of Our Lady of Kibeho. In his message, Bishop Misago says that "to celebrate worthily the Jubilee Year we must make concrete acts in the light of the message of Kibeho." Among them, he suggests: "praying during the year for all the intentions of the Pope; increasing participation at Mass and reception of Communion; receiving the sacrament of reconciliation." The bishop also urges "striving for reconciliation with enemies; asking forgiveness of people we have offended; respecting others;

	being tolerant in the family, with neighbors, at work, in meetings and other social events." To these gestures he adds "working with courage to promote truth and justice for all, particularly in present-day conditions of the Gacaca courts" -- peoples tribunals charged with judging persons accused of involvement in the 1994 genocide -- "which must be well managed to guarantee they do not become forums for injustice and revenge, covering the law." (Source: Zenit.org)
Nov 13, 2006	The Diocese of Gikongoro announced a Jubilee Year to celebrate the 25th anniversary of the Blessed Virgin Mary's first apparition in Kibeho. (Source: Zenit.org)
Nov 29. 2006	At the start of a jubilee year to mark the twenty-fifth anniversary of the first apparition, the Catholic bishops of Rwanda and Burundi led the celebrations attended by thousands of priests, men and women religious and lay people from Rwanda, Burundi, the Democratic Republic of Congo, Tanzania, Uganda and Europe. During the Mass, apostolic nuncio Archbishop

	Anselmo Guido Pecorari read a letter from Pope Benedict XVI announcing that a plenary indulgence had been granted by the apostolic penitentiary to pilgrims who visit Kibeho during the jubilee year. "Our Lady of Kibeho is a beacon of hope, a light for all Africa and the world. This was demonstrated by the fact that ten-thousand people braved torrential rain to take part in the ceremony to open the Kibeho jubilee year," Bishop Augustin Misago of Gikongoro, told the FIDES news service. "I was deeply moved at the devotion of the people taking part in the procession and the Mass which followed," Bishop Misago said. (Source: Catholic Information Service for Africa (CISA), 12/4/2006)
April 4, 2014	Meeting with the Rwandan bishops for their ad limina visit Thursday, Pope Francis urged them to be agents of reconciliation, commending them to the Marian apparition at Kibeho. "I commend you all to the maternal protection of the Virgin Mary," Pope Francis told the nation's bishops. "I sincerely

> hope that the Shrine of Kibeho might radiate even more the love of Mary for her children, especially the poorest and most injured, and be for the Church in Rwanda, and beyond, a call to turn with confidence to Our Lady of Sorrows, who accompanies each of us on our way that we might receive the gift of reconciliation and peace."
> (Source: Vatican.va "ADDRESS OF POPE FRANCIS TO THE BISHOPS OF THE EPISCOPAL CONFERENCE OF RWANDA ON THEIR AD LIMINA VISIT" 4/3/2014)

Messages and Visions:

In the visions, Mary emphasized the call to pray the rosary. She also asked for penance and fasting. A dreadful vision all three girls received became a key apparition leading to the official acceptance and approval of Kibeho.

These girls reported seeing a gruesome picture: a river of blood, people who killed one another, abandoned bodies with no one to bury them, a tree on fire, an open chasm, a monster, and severed heads. The vision is now considered a prophecy of the ethnic genocide that would take place in the country 13 years later. Tragically, in 1994, visionary Marie Claire became one of its victims.

Signs and Miracles:

From the beginning in Kibeho, in southern Rwanda, there were conversions, prayer meetings, pilgrimages, healings and abnormal phenomena during those public apparitions. Also, the sun appeared to pulsate, spin, or split in two — a miracle reminiscent of Fatima.

Description of the Virgin

"She had a seamless white dress and also a white veil on her head. Her hands were clasped together on her breast, and her fingers pointed to the sky... I could not determine the color of her skin," said Alphonsine, "but she was of incomparable beauty."

Approval

"Yes, the Virgin Mary did appear in Kibeho on Nov. 28, 1981," and then over "the course of the following six months," proclaimed Bishop Augustine Misago of Gikongoro, Rwanda, Africa, when he announced his official approval of the apparitions on June 29, 2001. "There are more reasons to believe this than to deny it."

He could not confirm the veracity of all the people who reported apparitions, however. Moreover, the document does not consider the alleged visions of Jesus, reported from 1982.

On July 2, 2001, the Holy See released the declaration of Bishop Augustin Misago of Gikongoro approving the apparitions.

The visions in Kibeho, Rwanda, are the most recently occurring Marian apparitions to receive official recognition by the Church. As early as 1982, an earlier bishop of the diocese, Bishop Jean Baptiste Gahamanyi, already authorized public devotion.

The feast of Our Lady of Kibeho is Nov. 28.

Appendix 10

Our Lady of the Rosary: San Nicolas, Argentina (1983)

(Note: This appendix is taken directly from EWTN's The Miracle Hunter website (http://www.miraclehunter.com) which gives a succinct timeline and description of the apparition and messages.)

Summary:

An ordinary housewife, a mother and grandmother who had no formal education and no knowledge of the Bible or theology claimed that she was visited by the Blessed Mother daily for a period of over 6 years. She reportedly additionally received 68 messages from Jesus Christ. Numerous healings, including the cure of a boy with a brain tumor, have been documented.

Timeline:

Sept 25, 1983	First appearance of the Virgin to Gladys Quiroga de Motta
Oct 7, 1983	Gladys asked the Virgin what she wanted. Gladys: "I saw her and I asked her what

	she wanted of me. Then her image faded away and a chapel appeared. I understood that she wanted to be among us."
Oct 12, 1983	Gladys discusses her experiences with a priest.
Oct 13, 1983	The Holy Virgin talks to her for the first time.
Nov 17, 1983	Gladys sprinkles holy water on the apparition.
Nov 19, 1983	Gladys is informed of her mission : "You will become the bridge of union. Proclaim my words."
Nov 24, 1983	A shaft of light in the darkness shows Gladys where the Church should be built - on a wasteland called Campito on the banks of the Parana river. The ray of light is seen by other witnesses, a nine-year old girl.
Nov 27, 1983	Gladys recognizes the apparition when she sees an image of the Lady of Rosary relegated to the belfry of the diocesan cathedral because of damage. The Virgin referred to Exodus 25;8 in describing the church to be built. The passage says, "They shall make a sanctuary for me, that I may dwell in their midst." The significance of the passage is that it contains the instructions given by God to the Israelites for building the Ark of the Covenant by means of which Yahweh would be present to them. The New Testament and the early Church has consistently understood Mary to be the New Ark of the Covenant, who was the dwelling place of the Holy Spirit

	and the Bearer of the Son. At San Nicolas, the Virgin was restating this teaching.
November 1984	Gladys is welcomed by the new bishop of San Nicolas, Domingo Salvador Castagna. The bishop has an audience with Pope John Paul II, at which he discusses the phenomenon.
April 1985	A Commission of Inquiry is named.
Feb 25, 1986	First pilgrimage and celebration of the Holy Mass in El Campito, the location of the new sanctuary.
May 25, 1986	Spreading of a medal introduced by the Virgin in the apparitions.
Sept 25, 1986	Placing of the foundation stone of the sanctuary.
April 11, 1987	Bishop Castagna has an audience with Pope John Paul II in Rosario, the main city of his diocese. The bishop promises the pope that he will direct a study of San Nicolas.
Oct 13, 1987	The building of the sanctuary begins.
March 19, 1989	Moving of the image from the cathedral and blessing and opening of the sanctuary.
Nov 1989	Bishop Castagna has another audience with the Pope.
Feb 11, 1990	The end of the catechesis of Our Lady of San Nicolas.
July 25, 1990	Bishop Castagna said: "Undoubtedly this event of grace will continue to grow; it has proved its authenticity by its spiritual fruits."

Aug 25, 1990	Bishop Castagna consecrates the sanctuary and the pilgrims to God through the Immaculate Heart of Mary.
Nov 14, 1990	The Bishop issued an edict comprising an "Imprimatur" for the publication of the Spanish edition of the Messages of Our Lady to Gladys de Motta.
Sep 28, 2008	Some 200,000 people participated in the Eucharistic celebration near the Sanctuary of Mary of the Rosary of San Nicolás, for the 25th Anniversary of the appearances of Our Lady in Argentina. The Eucharistic celebration was presided over by the Bishop of San Nicolás de los Arroyos, Héctor Cardelli who in his homily stressed that "when Mary calls us together, the family is reinforced, because the Mother is bringing her children together."
May 22, 2016	The apparitions of Our Lady of the Rosary were declared in a homily as having "supernatural in character" and "worthy of belief" by the local bishop, Most Rev. Hector Cardelli. He released the formal statement "La Escuela Espiritual de Santa Maria del Rosario de San Nicolas"
March 13, 2017	Mons. Hugo Santiago, Bishop of San Nicolas, Argentina, in a YouTube message, announced the stoppage of the publication of the messages currently being claimed by Gladys Motta de Quiroga until further review.

Description of the Virgin:

The Virgin's figure glowed with light. She had a blue gown and a veil and held the baby Jesus in her arms along with a large Rosary. She bore a close resemblance to a statue of Our Lady of the Rosary that had been left in the belfry of a nearby cathedral.

Messages:

More than eighteen hundred messages were given daily over the course of seven years were recognized as authentic. Further messages have bene reported in subsequent years and are under review by the Bishop of San Nicolas.

Miracles, Cures, and Signs:

Numerous healings, including the cure of a boy with a brain tumor, have been documented. Gladys could hardly read or write before the apparitions but somehow she was able to precisely document the messages. She received the stigmata on her wrists, feet, side and shoulder uniting her suffering to Lord as a victim soul.

Approval:

On July 25, 1990, the Bishop of San Nicolas, Monsignor Domingo Castagna said: "Undoubtedly this event of grace will continue to grow; it has proved its authenticity by its spiritual fruits."

On November 14, 1990, the Bishop issued an edict comprising an "Imprimatur" for the publication of the Spanish edition of the Messages of Our Lady to Gladys de Motta.

The Coming Era of Peace

On May 22, 2016, the apparitions of Our Lady of the Rosary were declared as having "supernatural in character" and "worthy of belief" by the local bishop, Most Rev. Hector Cardelli.

Appendix 11

VISION OF POPE LEO XIII AND THE PRAYER TO ST. MICHAEL

Although technically not a Marian apparition, there is a significant well-documented vision of Pope Leo XIII in the late 1800s that is of such historical importance that I have included it in this book. The vision and responding prayer are definitely predictive of our time.

The accounts of the vision vary and are included in a comprehensive book dealing with the event called *Pope Leo XIII and the Prayer to St. Michael*, written by Kevin Symonds in 2018.[47] Discussion of the vision of Pope Leo XIII is given on page 8 by Monsignor Carl Vogl, who himself was the author of the book "*Begone Satan: A Soul Stirring Account of Diabolical Possession in Iowa*" which took place in 1928. Msgr. Vogl referenced the vision of Pope Leo XIII as follows:

> Pope Leo XIII in our time composed a powerful and solemn prayer of exorcism for priests against

---

[47] Preserving Christian Publications, P.O. Box 221, Boonville, NY 13309-0221

the fallen angels and evil spirits. It is said that this pope, after God granted a vision of the great devastation Satan is carrying on in our times, composed the prayer of exorcism in honor of St. Michael that is now recited in the vernacular as one of the prayers after Mass.

The prayer that is being referred to is the St. Michael Prayer that most Catholics are very familiar with:

St. Michael, the archangel, defend us in the day of battle. Be our safeguard against the wickedness and snares of the devil. May God rebuke him, we humbly pray, and do thou, oh Prince of the Heavenly Host, by the divine power of God, cast into hell Satan and all evil spirits who roam throughout the world seeking the ruin of souls.
Amen.

Monsignor Vogl went on further and described one version of the Pope's vision as follows:

> A rather peculiar circumstance induced Pope Leo XIII to compose this powerful prayer. After celebrating Mass one day, he was in conference with the Cardinals. Suddenly he sank to the floor. Several doctors were summoned at once but found no sign of a pulse – the very life seemed to have ebbed away from the fragile and aging body. Suddenly he recovered and said, 'What a horrible vision I have been shown.' He saw the ages to come, the seductive powers and ravings of the devils against the Church in every land. But St. Michael appeared in the moment of greatest

distress and cast Satan and his cohorts back into the abyss of hell. Such was the occasion that caused Pope Leo XIII to prescribe this prayer for the universal church.

Another version of Pope Leo XIII's vision was elaborated by Padre Domenico Pechenino, the Major Rector of the Oblates beginning in 1919 and serving in this role through World War II.[48] He wrote an article in 1947 for the Italian newspaper[49] called, "The Tragedy of Our Times and the Work of Satan." He claimed to have knowledge of the vision of Pope Leo XIII and is quoted as follows:

> Then what happened? This is what happened. God had shown Satan to the vicar of his divine Son on earth, just like he did with Job. Satan was bragging that he had already devastated the Church on a large scale. In fact, these were tumultuous times for Italy, for many nations in Europe, and a bit around the world. The Freemasons ruled and governments hadn't become docile instruments. With the audacity of a boaster, Satan put a challenge to God. – 'And if you give me a little more freedom, you could see what I could do for your Church!' – 'What would you do?' – 'I would destroy it.' – 'Oh, that would be something to see. How long would it take?' – '50 or 60 years.' – 'Have more freedom and the time that you need, then we'll see what happens.'

---

[48] *Pope Leo XIII and the Prayer to St. Michael*, page 43
[49] 30 marzo, 1947, 2

Since these earlier reckonings, references to the vision of Pope Leo XIII have taken on a life of their own, especially with the advent of the Internet. Online accounts will indicate that Satan had a "guttural" voice, while the other voice was that of our Lord, which was more pleasant and kind. In addition, some online renderings of the account indicate that the timeframe that was requested by Satan was more in the 75 to 100 years range rather than the 50 to 60 years noted above. Other accounts indicate that the 20th century was given over to "Satan's power." Some have tried to tie the vison to the then upcoming apparition of Our Lady at Fatima indicating that the vision occurred specifically on October 13, 1884, exactly 33 years to the date prior to the Miracle of the Sun which occurred at Fatima on October 13, 1917.

In his comprehensive book on the subject noted previously, Kevin Symonds indicated that the historical evidence can only be taken so far. He noted that there was indeed a vision but that the actual date of the vision is in fact uncertain. He gave evidence that "it is not unreasonable to surmise that the vision may have taken place sometime between January 6, 1884, and August 1886..."[50]

He noted further in his conclusion the following paragraphs:

> We set out to examine the claim that Leo received a vision that was behind the composing of the prayer to St. Michael the Archangel. According to the best evidence now available, a vision did

---

[50] *Pope Leo XIII and the Prayer to St. Michael* written by Kevin Symonds in 2018 – page 31

precede this prayer and caused its composition. In looking at the evidence, we attempted to separate fact from fiction, truth from exaggeration. Some questions were answered while new ones are posed; still others must go unanswered.

Perhaps the most significant unanswered question is the alleged conversation between Jesus and Satan wherein the 20th century is given over to "Satan's power." For many, this account explained many riddles and difficulties in that century. While this part of the story is uncertain, one does not need private revelation to see the countless atrocities in the 20th century against the rights of God and of men. These atrocities reinforced but did not necessarily prove the various accounts of Leo's vision. Perhaps now, several years into the 21st century, with atrocities all its own, hindsight can better assist us.

Leo's vision was viewed as having an intimate association with the political and social upheaval of the day. This is consistent with Church teaching, that God sends such extraordinary graces to the faithful in order for them to live better the gospel in a particular moment of history. To this end, Pope Leo saw fit to compose the prayer to St. Michael and approve other prayers to the archangel for use among lay and ordained Catholics alike."[51]

---

[51] *Pope Leo XIII and the Prayer to St. Michael* written by Kevin Symonds in 2018 – page 131, note the copywrite of 2018

So for our purposes and according to the best evidence noted to be available as per Mr. Symonds, Pope Leo XIII did have a vision which preceded this prayer to St. Michael and caused its composition. Mr. Symonds indicated that it is not unreasonable for one to conclude that the vision occurred sometime between January 1884 and August 1886. We cannot be sure of any specific time frames or periods (i.e. the number of years) to which the vision is referencing. Nevertheless, a pope having a vision which affects him so much that he composes a prayer to St. Michael against Satan, to be utilized throughout the whole world, is in and of itself a noteworthy event.

Appendix 12

Consecration of Louis XVI, King of France, to the Sacred Heart of Jesus

"Well dost Thou see, O my God, the great sadness that oppresses my heart, the grief that wounds it and the depth of the abyss into which I have been cast. I am assailed by countless evils from all sides. To the oppression of my soul, the horrible tragedies that have befallen me and my family add up to those that cover the whole extension of the realm. The clamoring of all the misfortunate and the moans of our oppressed religion reaches my ears, and an inner voice suggests to me that perhaps Thy justice holds me accountable for all these calamities for not having restrained, during the days of my power, their main causes, which are the people's licentiousness and the spirit of irreligion, and for supplied heresy, now triumphant, its weapons by favoring it by laws that gave it redoubled strength and enough boldness to dare anything.

O Jesus-Christ! Divine Redeemer of all our iniquities, today I come to find relief for my soul in Thy Adorable Heart. I call to my aid the tender Heart of

Mary, my august protectress and Mother, and the assistance of Saint Louis, my advocate and the most illustrious of my ancestors. Open Thyself, adorable Heart, through the most pure hands of my powerful intercessors, receive benignantly the vows of which confidence inspires me and that I offer Thee as the frank expression of my sentiments. If, as a consequence of Divine goodness, I were to recover my liberty, my crown and royal power, I solemnly promise:

> 1. To revoke at once all the laws that will be indicated to me by the Pope, or a Council, or by four of the more learned and virtuous bishops of my realm, as contrary to the purity and the integrity of the Faith, and contrary to the discipline and the special jurisdiction of the Holy, Roman, Catholic, and Apostolic Church; and especially to revoke the Civil Constitution of the Clergy.
>
> 2. To take, within a year, all the necessary measures to establish, with the approval of the Pope and the episcopate of my realm, and in accordance with canonical standards, a solemn feast in honor of the Sacred Heart of Jesus to be celebrated forevermore throughout all France on the first Friday immediately after the eight days following the Feast of Corpus Christi and to be always followed by a general procession. This feast will be celebrated in reparation for the outrages and desecrations perpetrated in our holy temples by schismatics, heretics and the bad Christians in these times of so great turmoil.
>
> 3. To go in person on a Sunday or a holy day within three months of the day of my deliverance

to the Church of Notre Dame of Paris, or to any other principal church in the place where I will be at that time, to pronounce a solemn act of consecration of my person, my family and my realm to the Sacred Heart of Jesus next to the main altar after the Offertory of the Mass and through the hands of the priest, promising to give to all my vassals an example of the worship and the devotion due that adorable Heart.

4. To erect and adorn within a year of my release and at my own expense, in the church that I will choose, a chapel or an altar to be dedicated to the Sacred Heart, which will stand as a lasting monument of my recognition and limitless confidence in the infinite merits and inexhaustible treasures of grace that this Divine Heart contains.

5. Finally, to renew every year, wherever I might be on the Feast of the Sacred Heart, the act of consecration stated in the third point and to participate in the general procession that will take place right after that day's Mass.

Now I cannot pronounce this pact except in secret, but I would sign it with my own blood if necessary; and the most beautiful day of my life will be when I will be able to proclaim it aloud in the Temple.

O Adorable Heart of my Savior, may I neglect my right hand and my own being if I were to ignore Thy benefits these my promises, if I were to cease to love Thee and place all my trust and comfort in Thee! Amen."

— Louis XVI, King of France

About the Author

David G Smithson, MD, has been practicing for over 30 years as a rehabilitation medicine physician. He holds degrees from Saint Mary's University of Minnesota, the University of Minnesota and the University of Washington. He is a life-long Catholic and resides in the Kansas City area with his wife, Mollie, of 38 years where they raised their five children. Dr. Smithson's other Catholic related books include *The Parable of White Fang*, based on the classic Jack London novel (2021) and *Prayer or Mantra, A Contrast between Christian Prayer and Eastern Meditation* (2006).

(Every effort was made in the research undertaken to be truthful and transparent. In the end, it is deferred to church theologians, historians and pastors to analyze the statements and opinions thus generated.)

www.ingramcontent.com/pod-product-compliance
Lightning Source LLC
Chambersburg PA
CBHW071341080526
44587CB00017B/2913